Praise for Aw

I've known Sid Webb for 30 years, and have benefited greatly from his wisdom, encouragement, and heart. *Awake from Bible Slumber* is your opportunity to learn with him as he helps you unlock the essential message of the Bible for yourself.
—**PHIL TUTTLE, President, Walk Thru the Bible Ministries.**

My friend Sid Webb has created a unique and very special "Bible story" that enables us to understand Scripture more easily and gain a clearer perspective for a more personal and practical application of God's message. It's going to be a powerful, fun, and exciting learning tool for all.
—**COLONEL LEE ELLIS, USAF (Ret), President, Leadership Freedom; Former POW; Author of the award-winning** *Leading with Honor: Leadership Lessons from the Hanoi Hilton* **and** *Captured by Love: Inspiring True Romance Stories from Vietnam POWs.*

Sidney Webb is a gifted Bible scholar who has been used to illuminate the truth of God's Word in practical ways to many different audiences. He has the unique ability to communicate in a way that presents scriptural truths with clarity, hope, and theological rigor. This book is a valuable tool to help us all grow in the knowledge and understanding of God's grace and redemption.
—**DR. DANE EGLI, Senior Advisor, Ministry of Defense, Kingdom of Saudi Arabia.**

This compilation is a rich resource to add to any Bible student's library. The possibilities for opening our hearts and minds to greater insight are unlimited. The methods for in-depth Bible study that Sid includes are thought-provoking and challenging.

—CAMILLA LEATHERS SEABOLT, Former Executive Director, Community Bible Study.

I'm so grateful for this book. For parents, for leaders, for students, for new believers, for spiritually interested folks. Sid brings clarity and inspiration through his words. Having sat under his teaching and mentorship for decades, and having witnessed the deep understanding of the Bible that his students, mentees, audiences, and readers have enjoyed, I know firsthand the power of his story-telling and questioning methods. If you're like me in looking for encouragement in troubled times and simplicity amidst complexity, then this book is for you.

—DR. TYLER THIGPEN, Head of The Forest Schools and Academic Director at the University of Pennsylvania Graduate School of Education.

Sid Webb has decades of bringing the Bible's story to life for people of all ages through his fun, accessible, innovative approach. Sid's guidance through the Scriptures radically changed my life many years ago, and I can't wait for *Awake from Bible Slumber* readers to similarly meet God's Word in a fresher, more profound way.

—JACOB DAVIS, Editor, *The Anglican Compass*.

Every reader will benefit from following the trail Dr. Sid marks out to lead us deeper into God's Word.

—TODD NETTLETON, Host, *The Voice of the Martyrs Radio*; Author of the award-winning *When Faith is Forbidden: 40 Days on the Frontlines with Persecuted Christians*.

I've never seen the inmates in my prison respond to the Bible quite the way they did when we implemented Sid's methods and they acted out Jesus washing the feet of his disciples. It was a fun and simple approach to group Bible study that helped the story stick and reveal the truths in the passage.

—ALICIA REEVES, Chaplain, La Vista Correctional Facility, Pueblo, Colorado.

The numbers have been clear for some years now: Lots of Bibles sold, but many fewer Bibles actually read. This book can surely help individuals, groups, and churches reverse that last statement. I've known and respected Dr. Sid Webb for several years now. His knowledge of Scriptures is extensive. His passion for Christ is strong, He's a terrific writer (see his book *Nomad's Fire*), and a born teacher. I very much look forward to using this book in our church.

—REV. MATT BURNETT, Pastor, Holy Trinity Anglican Church.

God's word is eternal and true. It never changes, and it is always relevant. It is the sure foundation we can rely on, no matter what else is happening in our lives. It is the light to our path. To neglect the word of God is to abandon the very thing that has the power to change our lives both here and in eternity. This resource may help you grasp and apply it for the first time—and forever.

—WALT LARIMORE, MD, Internationally-recognized family physician, educator, and award-winning, best-selling author of *The Best Medicine: Tales of Humor and Hope from a Small-Town Doctor*; *The Best Gift: Tales of a Small-Town Doctor Learning Life's Greatest Lessons*; and, *At First Light: A True World War II Story of a Hero, His Bravery, and an Amazing Horse.*

Awake from Bible Slumber is an incredible Bible resource that helps the reader resolve their confusion in order to understand and delight in the Bible more. With Dr. Webb's extensive knowledge and love of the Bible combined with his ability to make it practically accessible to everyone, this is a resource that will help anyone realize they can understand and apply the Bible to their life. What a powerful resource for individuals, churches, organizations, and every Bible-reader's shelf!

—KRISTIN NAVE, Author and Founder of *All Things Bible*.

We have not been given a book of verses; we have been given a story written by a loving Father. An entire generation growing up in the church has slept through the story. For over 20 years, I have been blessed by the creative teaching, discipleship, and leadership of Dr. Sid Webb. I have never seen him put anyone to sleep! This will be fun.

—DR. RANDY RAINWATER, Grace New Hope Campus Pastor; Grace Network Pastor of Students.

You get what you concentrate on. Dr. Webb has concentrated on helping others access the Bible's message. I'm glad he did. And I am especially glad he is sharing all he learned in *Awake from Bible Slumber*. Get it, read it, and you will be too!

—MIKE WAGNER, Dallas Theological Seminary; Founder, White Rabbit Group.

If there was ever a book that needed to be written for the masses, this is it. Many people are hungering for the guidance that can only come from God's Word, but Satan has convinced them that it is indecipherable. Dr. Webb makes the most relevant book (the Bible) accessible to anyone who really wants to read the Scriptures for meaning.

—GORDON DASHER, Writer and Pastor, Swannanoa Christian Church.

Awake from Bible Slumber is a wall-blaster for sure! Too many Christians rely on the "professionals" to explain the Bible. Not any more! Dr. Webb lays it out, through all 66 Books, in a fun and interactive, easy-to-understand way... your Bible will make sense and come alive like never before!

—**STEVE McAULEY, Pastor, Word Fellowship; Representative, All Pro Dad.**

Immersion in the study of God's word is essential in understanding God's ways and His purpose for each of us in our life on earth. His word teaches how to live in our complex world.

—**BRIGADIER GENERAL MASON CROWE, US Army (Ret).**

Sid has a knack for removing the barriers that have been getting in your way of fully experiencing the gift of the Scriptures. No "wah wah wah" every time you open the Bible. *Awake from Bible Slumber* is an incredible tool that will open your eyes and heart to the gift of the Scriptures.

—**HEATHER FISHER, Family Life Radio.**

Dr. Sidney Webb brings the stories of the Bible to life in a comprehensible way using a method that is informative beyond anything I have ever studied or read. He does this with a passion and knowledge that makes him a master at his craft. He is a true Steward of God.

—**TERRIE JORDAN, *AfBS* participant.**

Dr. Sidney Webb's years of experience, passion to teach and preach God's word invites AfBS readers to grasp the Bible in a creative manner with practical creative study methods that both honour integrity to the text at the same time relevant to our situations today. A great book that ignites every heart and mind to live a Christ-centered life by applying!

MAGARAJA PRASANTH, Andhra Pradesh, India. Pastor, Maranatha Temple.

The excellent content in this book will motivate you to deepen your relationship with God as Sid shows you from the Bible His faithfulness to all generations (Psalm 100:5b).

—**DELBERT TUXHORN, The Navigators.**

Awake from Bible Slumber is filled with meaningful, systematic content along with supplemental maps and charts to make Bible Study fresh and exciting. Dr. Webb's experience and personality join to create a "not to be missed" volume for interactive personal or group study.

—**NANCY GHEESLING, College of Education, University of North Georgia; Adult Discipleship leader, First Baptist Ellijay.**

When learning is fun, you want to share (or give away) all that you learn. That is when discipleship becomes alive and real. Sid's enthusiasm and energy in teaching the Bible is contagious. But more importantly is the life he leads. I have personally watched him disciple others in nonprofit boards and Bible study small groups. He makes studying the Bible fun and joyful. *Awake from Bible Slumber* will encourage you, motivate you, and create joy in Bible study.

—**DANNY SPINKS, Chair, Grace Family of Churches; Former Chair, Grace Fellowship Church and the Brookwood Christian Learning Center; Former Pastor, Grace Marietta.**

In a remarkable demonstration of God weaving people together in spiritually enriching relationships, I have been honored to share three seasons of my life journey with Dr. Sid Webb. From visiting New York City together while in grad school, working alongside each other in Asia ten years later, and eventually sharing ministry platforms around the US, I have been inspired and challenged by Sid's skill at understanding and expressing deep spiritual insights. This book is birthed from Sid's lifetime of study and a vast array of experiences. *Awake from Bible Slumber* will open new doors of understanding and perspective on the most important and influential book in history. Let the Word come alive!

—DR. JASON PETERS, Chaplain (Lieutenant Colonel) USAF (Ret); Founder, EPICly.

Dr. Webb has written a concise primer on Biblical exegesis and proper Bible study. Unlike those who believe that the Bible must be altered to become relevant, he shows how the Bible can come alive because it is relevant. He takes us through the Bible and gives us tools to follow.

—DR. DAVID CRISWELL, producer/director/writer of the award-winning film *Voice of the Dead*; author of the *Biblical Controversies* series.

I am so excited to see the work Sid Webb is putting out to help everyone enjoy and explore the Bible—we have no better authority for this life than the Scriptures and anything that makes it come alive for the reader I'm an advocate for!

REV. STACY DYER, Associational Missionary for the Morganton and Mountaintown Baptist Associations.

Awake from Bible Slumber

Awake from Bible Slumber

How to Make the Word Come Alive

Sidney A. Webb

Published by Sharpened Focus
3472 Research Parkway, Ste. 104-635
Colorado Springs, Colorado 80920
www.sharpenedfocus.com
info@sharpenedfocus.com

Awake from Bible Slumber: How to Make the Word Come Alive

ISBN 978-1-7321576-3-7 *Paperback*

ISBN 978-1-7321576-5-1 *Ebook PUB*

ISBN 978-1-7321576-4-4 *Ebook Kindle*

1 2 3 4 5 6 7 8 9 10

Dedicated to Suzy Webb, fellow hiker on the journey.

Contents

They read from the book, from the Law of God, clearly, and they gave the sense, so that the people understood the reading.
—Nehemiah 8:8

.

Introduction: You Can Understand The Bible

"You see all this cool stuff in the Bible, but we can't see anything. How do you do it?"

I expected this question from my high school students. What blew me away was when adults would ask me the same thing. I assumed the adults had been around long enough to figure it out.

Can you relate to their struggle? Over the years, many people have told me that when they look at the Bible, they see a black-and-white "wall of words." The pages of Scripture are impenetrable to them. Seminary taught me to mine the Scriptures, including the original Hebrew and Greek, to find the gold. But the vast majority of people are not going to have that experience. And while there are great inductive Bible study programs such as Community Bible Study, Precept, and Bible Study Fellowship, most people have not participated.

And, let's face it, reading the Bible is a challenge. The Bible contains 66 books written by dozens of authors over 1,500 years. It describes events from the dawn of creation to the eternal kingdom. It tells of thousands of characters and multitudes of social and cultural environments.

The Bible contains crazy incidents, miracles, apocalyptic disasters, appearances of God and Satan, and the presence of both good angels and demons. At the book's heart is a man who claimed to be God, got killed for it, and rose from the dead. It's no wonder you're overwhelmed!!! I wrote this book to help you better grasp all of it.

To get things out of the Bible, do you have to undergo extensive training, or can you start gleaning nuggets *now*? I believe you can begin to deepen your Bible understanding *today*. This book will guide you into it.

God has given you a brain and the ability to see, perceive, and reason. He has hardwired a love for story in you. And you can read! You already have a foundation for Bible study; what you need is for someone to show you what to look for. And that's what this book is about. I designed it to help you use things you already know to equip you to read what may seem confusing.

The *Awake from Bible Slumber* (*AfBS*) idea began taking on shape when I saw that the "wall of words" issue was a problem for people of *all ages*. And it gained traction when I studied to produce dramas for church worship services. The process of analyzing characters and staging had great relevance to Bible study.

I threw together some ideas for the initial version of AfBS, a three-day retreat for high school and college students in 2004. At the time, I called it *Making the Bible Come Alive*. It was an experiment, and they were the guinea pigs. The result blew me away. The retreat experience *far* exceeded expectations. It hit all of us with lightning bolts of insight. According to Hebrews 4:12, the Bible is already alive, but we were watching it spring to life in our midst.

In the ensuing years, I continued to deliver (what I now call) *Awake from Bible Slumber* in various settings and lengths of time. I taught it to high school classes for a week. I used it for weekly adult Sunday School. During Covid, I produced a Facebook Live version that drew hundreds of viewers. But all along, I was nagged by the thought that I should develop a book and systematize the process. This book is the result.

AfBS has infinite potential for impact. It is also highly adaptable. I have written with flexibility in mind; you may cover the material from many angles, as I'll explain in the next chapter. The material will help you in your individual Bible study, sure. But I'm also giving you a powerful tool for a Sunday School class, a weekly Bible study, or a retreat. Follow the process, and your group will experience dynamic results.

In the next chapter, we'll dig into the *AfBS* approach—how to explore the details and mine the gold of the Bible. We'll introduce techniques that make the Bible sprout before you. After that, I'll give ideas for both individual and group study to prime your mental pump.

Later in the book, you'll find a simple, user-friendly Bible overview. Most people have never had one. Watch your mental lights switch on! The chapter includes maps and charts to clarify the big picture. The chapter after the overview contains a summary of every book in the Bible. With those chapters, the Bible will make more sense to you.

After that are two unique chapters. One is a Theological Dictionary to help you track with terms you might hear in church. The other is a chapter on the incarcerated in the Bible. I included it to encourage our brothers and sisters who are behind bars; God is doing great work in their lives, but they face intense challenges and spiritual warfare.

Again, you can do it! You have the Holy Spirit and what you need within to make the Bible come alive in front of you. Let's start!

Part One
A Way to Make Your Bible Study Come Alive

A Way to Make Your Bible Study Come Alive

Let's look at how to explore the Bible in an engaging, even fun, way.

The heart of *Awake from Bible Slumber* is a set of 15 words. Each word is a theme that represents an eye-opening method of looking at Scripture.

I'll describe each word and how it makes the Bible come alive. In this chapter, I list the 15 words and their definitions. The following chapters will guide you through understanding and using each word. Each chapter includes Scripture examples and suggested Scriptures for you to study yourself.

For example, after reading the sequence chapter, you'll notice the presence of "sequence" every time you read the Bible. You'll follow the flow of Bible stories and teachings. And you'll have some clues as to how you might apply the passages.

I have designed *Awake from Bible Slumber* to stimulate your creative thinking. The key to understanding it is to realize it is highly flexible and adaptable; you can use this program in several ways, each worthy in its own right. Will you work through it independently or with a class or group? How much time do you have available? What's the knowledge level of the attendees? No matter how you approach it, you will benefit.

You can use this program in person or online (Facebook Live, YouTube, etc.). You can meet for one session or an entire semester. You can go through it as an individual. One of the best ways is with an in-person group. You can lead your family or a homeschool group through it. It's great for a youth program, a Bible study, or a Sunday School class. My colleagues are using it weekly in a women's prison Bible study.

AfBS also makes for a fabulous weekend retreat! On a retreat, I explain the ideas and guide you through them interactively. It's a lot of fun; everyone will see something new, even the leader! Please get in touch with me if you'd like me to lead your study or retreat. Contact me at info@sharpenedfocus.com or use the contact form at www.sharpenedfocus.com.

Below is a listing of the words (a.k.a. steps) in the *AfBS* process. In the following chapters, I'll explain each in detail and give you some Scriptures that cause it to sprout and bear fruit.

SUPPLICATE
Begin your study by praying for God to give you insight into the passage.

SOAK
Read the passage (and only it) several times to let it saturate.

SEEK
Ask questions about it (who, what, when, where, why, and how).

SEE
Observe the passage, looking for things you never noticed before.

STORY
A dramatic or humorous narrative that interests or instructs.

SCENE

A story segment describing what happens between characters.

STEP

A bit of action or dialogue which moves the story ahead; it's a moment of change.

STARS

The characters. Each has goals, emotions, behaviors, and a life background.

STAGING

The placement and movement of characters in the scene.

SPECKS

Noticing the details of the structure (starting with the verbs).

SITE

Where the story takes place, and what makes the location significant.

SETTING

The biblical, historical, cultural, and immediate context.

SEQUENCE

The words of timing and logical flow.

SPEAKING

The insight that comes from sounding out the passage and even changing emphasis.

SPARK

Considering the principles of the passage, and how you can apply them in your life.

~

Okay, so we have 15 words/steps. What do we do with them?

One fantastic way is to use the 15 words as the **skeleton for a course, class, or semester**, such as a Bible study or Sunday School class. You could lead one session per step and work through all of them in the course. That's 15 weeks. But "supplicate" is the first word, and I assume you'll always pray before each session, so you could go through the material in fourteen weeks.

You could **adjust the material to fit the number of sessions available**. For example, if you have six sessions, double up on the words. But some chapters are long enough that you may need to spend two or more sessions on them. The beauty of this system is that it flexes with your needs. Do what works best for you!

Another approach is to **move through the detail steps (soak, seek, see, site, setting, etc.) first, and only after that, head toward the story steps**. This approach is more academic and will work best with an audience used to detail and inductive Bible study. It works less well with unbelievers, new believers, believers untrained in inductive Bible study, less educated people, and the very young.

Another way is to "flip the sequence," **starting with the story steps and then working into the detail steps (speck)**. What that does is capitalize on people's fascination with stories. Drama is a universal concept. Once people are captivated by the story and think more deeply about how it plays out, they will naturally hunger for the details.

This fabulous approach works very well with younger people, unbelievers, new believers, and the less educated. And the mature like it, too! It's the heart of what I designed *Awake from Bible Slumber* to be: Moving people from seeing the Bible as a "black and white wall of words" to a living thing. The secret is getting people to observe the story. Some people like to be "on the stage," giving you a chance to get those personalities in front of the group to act out the story. The other ones will guide and correct them on the details. The audience gleans parts and principles from the word and then figures out how to use them to honor God and grow spiritually.

You can also gain tremendous value by **selecting only a few words** and working through them. Say, for instance, you have two teaching sessions and need some content. Pick one word for each session, or choose a few words to cover more briefly in each session. The story words are great for this.

It's often not possible to teach a semester-long course. You may have only a few sessions available. You don't want to rush through the *AfBS* system, so what do you do? First, don't stress about it! *Awake from Bible Slumber* has power and flexibility. You can be flexible without losing the power.

You have to realize that each step is worthy and useful in its own right. If you are short on time, **pick out one step and focus on it**. For example, I love to show people the concept of sequence. If they grasp "sequencing," it revolutionizes their Bible study. The chapter on speaking is fun because people get to perform different intonations. The story chapter is hugely compelling. You could do a whole series on stars and staging. You get the idea.

The bottom line is that you don't have to be concerned if you don't have much time. Leverage the steps in the most impactful way for your crowd. There's no right or wrong way to go through this program; you might like some words better than others. What's your favorite way to approach the material? It's better to do a few than nothing!

Part Two
Look More Closely

Chapter 1
Supplicate: Prayer

To supplicate is to begin your study by praying for God to give you insight into the passage.

Hear instruction and be wise, and do not neglect it. Blessed is the one who listens to me, watching daily at my gates, waiting beside my doors.
—Proverbs 8:33-34

Why do we study the Bible?

The Bible is one of God's greatest gifts to us. Seek its truths, and they will reward you with encouragement and insight. Its pages abound with words of life and hope. They infuse you with wonder. The word flows over you with nourishment and comfort. At times, it prods you with conviction.

As the Creator of the Universe speaks, we feel his heartbeat. We learn of his sovereign design and infinite power. We witness his immense love for his creatures. We vividly see how he expressed that love by giving his Son for our salvation.

You can sense spiritual energy in the Bible. Hebrews 4:12 says that the "word of God is living and active, sharper than any two-edged sword, piercing to the division of soul and of spirit, of joints and of marrow, and discerning the thoughts and intentions of the heart." The Bible slices and dices with purpose.

I once heard that most of our prayers are basically complaints about how God is running the world. Let's turn that around by using our prayer time to stimulate positive growth. God is waiting for you to pray with determination before he opens your mind to his truth. As you prepare to examine the Bible, then, begin with dedicated prayer. Pray that:

- You will be able to focus. Pray that your mind will be clear and that God will bat away distractions.
- You will be refreshed with God's love and grace.
- You will draw closer to God.
- Your thoughts of worry will dissolve.
- You will look at the word without bias but with a spirit of seeking what God has for you.
- You will have noteworthy observations and insights.
- You will have clarity on how to live out what you see in the word. That your attitudes and behavior will become ever more Christ-like.
- If your heart is hard, God will soften it.

In other words, may your heart echo with joy the words of Psalm 119:97-105:

Oh how I love your law! It is my meditation all the day.
Your commandment makes me wiser than my enemies, for it is ever with me.
I have more understanding than all my teachers,
for your testimonies are my meditation.
I understand more than the aged, for I keep your precepts.
I hold back my feet from every evil way, in order to keep your word.

I do not turn aside from your rules, for you have taught me.
How sweet are your words to my taste, sweeter than honey to my mouth!
Through your precepts I get understanding; therefore I hate every false way.
Your word is a lamp to my feet and a light to my path.

The word is our light! Now let's flip the switch!

Chapter 2
Soak: Absorption

T*o soak is to read the passage (and only it) several times to let it saturate.*

To soak is to absorb. Absorption takes a steady supply of liquid and a willing receptacle (think sponge!). Squeeze a sponge in water, and it will become completely wet. When you wring it out, you get what was absorbed, right? What comes out of *you* when you are "wrung out"? Absorb the Scriptures, and you should ooze the word when squeezed. (Easier said than done!)

I lived on the Gulf Coast of Florida, where getting three inches of rain at a time was not unusual. I developed a rain scale to help me adapt to the weather. On a scale of 1-5, one was drizzle, and five meant you better call Noah. I've occasionally been in 4-5 level storms, but steady rains tend to be 2-3. A shower of level one will gradually get you wet. A three will soak you in a couple of minutes. A four or five will drench you inside and out. With a five, frogs hop out of your pockets.

Soaking is an essential process in Bible study. With soaking, we read a passage multiple times. At first, we don't see much, but gradually the insights flow. Using the rain scale illustration, when we say that the Bible is a "wall of words" to us, we see it at a "one" level. We haven't absorbed much. Let's aim to get you up to a soak level of four or five, where you have the word on your mind and are growing in your ability to understand it.

Soaking begins with choosing to take the time necessary to absorb the Scriptures. If it has not been a habit before, you must make it one. When you intend to build a habit, you must find a trigger for it. Find something to remind you to open the word and soak it in. What can you use as a regular cue in your schedule to prompt you? Can you cue yourself by choosing to be in the word with your morning or afternoon coffee? Or before breakfast? Or when things settle down in the evening?

HOW TO SOAK

Soak is related to *supplication* and *Spirit*. As we said in the chapter on "supplication," pray fervently that the Holy Spirit would open the passage to your understanding.

Ask God to help filter out all distractions and surface insights as you read. Find a quiet spot and read the word several times while giving your full attention. Meditate on it over and over. Start with a small portion of Scripture before going to larger chunks.

Forget multitasking; single-task the word of God. Turn off your phone, screen out the distractions, put away your email, and go face-to-face with God's message. Perhaps even photocopy or print only the section you want to read and remove all surrounding verses. It takes time and focus to have something soak in. Let the word sink in, and see if you don't start noticing new insights.

One way to help you soak in the word is to listen to it. Try a Bible audio if you learn best by hearing or don't read well. There's nothing shameful about it; missions organizations are spreading audio Bibles worldwide, because many cultures are oral in nature.

(We'll discuss this more in the speaking chapter.) Audio recordings, such as those by Max McLean or *The Bible Experience*, will help you to soak in more. Listen to a passage a few times, and things start to pop out.

Using the soak method, I uncovered some excellent insights on Ephesians recently. I realized how frequently Paul used the words "all" or "every" (both are from the Greek term *pas*). Paul had conviction about God's nature and what he has done for us. One example is when he said, *God and Father of our Lord Jesus Christ . . . has blessed us in Christ with every spiritual blessing in the heavenly places* (1:3). *Every* is *pas*.

When I give Bible readings in our church service, I use the soak process to help me know how to express them. I read the passage repeatedly until I grasp it better and choose what syllables to emphasize. Soak always reveals new insights.

A SCRIPTURE TO PRACTICE ON

You could try this with Scriptures all over the Bible, but why don't you practice with Paul's magnificent statement in Ephesians 2:8-10? Take time to soak it in. Read it five or ten times. Listen to it several times. (Have someone read it to you, or use an audio Bible.) What comes to mind as you absorb the words?

PARTING THOUGHTS

It takes a while to absorb new things. We often miss things because we pass by them so quickly. When you glide quickly through a Scripture, you'll miss the more profound and meatier things.

A "sound bite" society has to put in extra work to absorb the nutrition of the Scriptures. Give plenty of time for the word to soak in. Start with one verse. Then move on to larger chunks of Scripture.

Focus has become a scarce commodity in our tech-oriented, busy society. That has dinged our ability to process the word of God. Determine to rediscover the power of focus in your life. Take time for God's word. Soak should open up insights and draw you closer to God.

Chapter 3
Seek: Questioning

T o seek is to ask questions about the passage (who, what, when, where, why, and how).

So Pilate entered his headquarters again and called Jesus and said to him, 'Are you the King of the Jews?' Jesus answered, 'Do you say this of your own accord, or did others say it to you about me?'
—*John 18:33-34*

THE POWER OF QUESTIONS

If we're going to understand the Bible, we have to see and comprehend new things.

There is power in seeing what you haven't seen before. The biblical "aha moment" sizzles your spiritual nerve endings. How do you get the ball rolling? By asking questions. Questions unearth gold nuggets of information. Sir Francis Bacon said that *A prudent question is one half of wisdom.*

If you feel stuck in the mud with your understanding of the

Bible, perhaps it is because you're not asking enough questions about the passage you're viewing. Or, maybe you are not asking the best questions.

When we ask good questions, we engage the recipient in a conversation. We encourage the person to think. Questions invite her, in an unthreatening way, to engage with the issues and go deeper than what she only "sees." With a question, you are not lecturing but drawing her into the quest for an answer. So I'll use many questions when I'm encouraging people to grow spiritually.

That works person to person. In this chapter, though, we are talking about one-sided questions that a person may ask about an inanimate object: A sheet of Scripture. The idea is still similar; asking questions causes us to see and learn things we haven't seen before. And you multiply the power of the process if you involve a group in asking the questions.

YOU'LL FIND QUESTIONS ALL OVER THE BIBLE

Jesus was a Master at asking questions himself. He knew their power. You could say that he was a superior coach who used them as some of his greatest tools. The questions engaged people, drawing them in. See, for example, the many questions he asked in John 3-4. And how did he use questions in John 18:28-40, interacting with Pilate?

With questions, Jesus exposed the truth. I analyzed Jesus's use of questions and found that he asked over 300 of them. The pattern of his questions was fascinating; he tended to play "verbal volleyball," using questions to set people up for His point. Bump, set, SMASH!

The Bible contains many classic questions, such as:

- *Where are you?* (said by God to Adam and Eve)
- *Have you eaten of the tree of which I commanded you not to eat?* (again, God to Adam and Eve)

- *Who told you you were naked?* (God to Adam and Eve)
- *What is truth?* (Pilate to Jesus)
- *My God, My God, why have You forsaken Me?* (Psalm 22, and Jesus on the cross)
- *Do you love Me?* (Jesus to Peter, after Peter had denied Him)
- *Saul, why are you persecuting Me?* (Jesus to Paul, on the Damascus Road)
- *Who are you, Lord?* (Paul's response)
- *Lord, will you at this time restore the kingdom to Israel?* (the disciples to Jesus right before he ascended to heaven)
- *Men of Galilee, why do you stand looking into heaven?* (what the disciples heard from the angels after Jesus ascended)

WHAT QUESTIONS SHOULD YOU ASK ABOUT THE BIBLE?

One can use questions to gather facts or to explore ideas. Bible study includes both. Be sure to ask plenty of *open-ended* questions. Here's a tip: If you're stuck, ask a question that starts with *What*. This technique works with the Bible, and it also works with our fellow humans.

Let's expand on that a bit. You've probably heard of the "Journalistic Questions," the ones reporters use to research and write a story. It so happens that these questions are beneficial for Bible study.

The idea behind the "journalistic questions" is that the reporter must give the significant facts upfront so the viewers won't be frustrated by not getting their immediate questions answered. A good article will therefore get to the main points right away, ensuring that the journalistic questions are covered. **The Journalistic Questions** are:

- Who was involved? (Who did it, or to whom was it done?)

- What happened?
- When did it happen?
- Where did it happen?
- Why did it happen?
- How did it happen?

Looking at Scripture, we ask: Who are the people in this passage? What is happening in this passage? Where is this story taking place? When does it occur (day, year, history, etc.)?

Asking the questions can help you notice terms and identify the mood. The answers will also enable you to use your imagination to recreate the scene you're reading about.

As you answer the questions and imagine the event, you'll probably come up with more questions. Asking those additional questions for understanding will help to build a bridge between observation (the first step) and interpretation (the second step) of the Bible study process.

Let's consider how you could use questions in the passage before you:

WHO

- Who is in the passage?
- Who is the hero? (Or is there one?)
- Who is the enemy?
- Who is the focal point?
- Who is the audience in the story, watching what is going on?
- Is the story for the watchers?

WHAT

- What is happening?
- What is the purpose of the encounter/exchange/story?
- What are the steps/narrative beats? (More on that in another chapter.)
- What are the points at which things shift or change?
- What might be the purpose of this passage in the Bible? (What part does it play in the writer's argument?)
- What is the outcome of the story? (What result does the story produce in the characters, the scene, the context, etc.)

WHEN

- When do things shift? (Such as when the light goes on for a character, when a character shuts down insight from others, when a decision is made, when an action is taken, etc.)
- When did this story or book take place?
- When did the event take place in the story of humanity?
- When does it take place in the story of the Bible?
- When in the history of Israel?
- When in the life of Jesus?
- When in the history of the church?

WHERE

- Where did it take place? Stories in the Bible can take place anywhere from a major country to an outhouse. Maybe it happened in the temple or on a mountain,

lake, or river. Was it a village? City? Country? Province?
A room in a house? An upper room?

- Sometimes, asking where it did *not* take place is helpful.
  (In other words, maybe you'd expect it to occur
  somewhere in particular, but it takes place elsewhere.
  For example, Jesus often has serious conversations in
  party-type situations rather than the synagogue.)

WHY

- Why might this event have happened? Find *possible*
  reasons, but don't fixate on finding *the* reason.
- Why might this story be in the Bible? (Of the millions
  of things the Bible could have included, only a select few
  were. What's there must be significant.)

HOW

- How is it recorded? What type of literature is this
  passage: Narrative (story), poetry, preaching, a listing of
  names (genealogies)?
- How do things happen?
- How do characters "shift" (change)?
- How does conflict break out?
- How do things resolve? (Or, do they? Are they left
  hanging?)

PRACTICING THE POWER OF QUESTIONS

Now, let's apply the power of asking questions on a Bible passage. Look at John 2:1-11, the story of Jesus's first miracle. Several questions come to mind with the first five verses alone:

- What is the significance of "the third day"?
- Where is Cana?
- Why is Jesus up there?
- Where is Jesus's dad?
- Did the family of Jesus know the bride and groom?
- Why was Jesus invited?
- Why did Mary (mother of Jesus) tell him out of the blue that they had no wine?
- Why does Jesus seem to respond belligerently in v. 4?
- How does his mother know he has this power? How does she know that the servants should do whatever he tells them?

For extra credit, ask why the first miracle of Jesus is to take water and turn it into wine!

To practice the power of questions independently, pick a passage with five-to-ten verses and use the Journalistic Questions on it. See what happens!

THE TICKLISH ISSUE OF ASKING GOD QUESTIONS

Everyone I know has many questions about God and for God. We're all trying to figure things out. Most people are wondering what their next step is in God's plan. Many are wondering why God isn't (or doesn't appear to be) answering their prayers. Humans are finite, but God is infinite. He claims sovereign authority. So, why wouldn't we have plenty of questions? The God who created us understands that.

Many people are nervous about asking questions regarding God and the Bible for fear that God will bring down his hammer of judgment. Also, we tend to stay in our comfort zones and stick with our tried-and-true opinions and answers. We don't want to have our beliefs or assumptions challenged. But the Bible has infinite room for questions. Every verse can prompt multiple questions. And God can undoubtedly handle your questions; if anyone has the answers, he does!

From my experience, God loves it when humans ask him questions. It means we are "still in the game" with him, wanting to know his will and caring about the direction of our lives.

It's one thing to ask questions of God and another thing to defy him. Challenging him may cross the line and become disrespectful. But, again, it may show that you care. Throughout the centuries, he has engaged with people who challenge him. Classic cases include the story of Job or Jacob in the all-night wrestling match with God. The worst thing for a person is when he doesn't care enough to try. (Look at the eye-opening message God gave the church at Laodicea in Revelation 3; he told them that he'd rather they be hot or cold than lukewarm.) My point is that you should take your concerns to God rather than avoiding him.

PARTING THOUGHTS

There is power in seeing what you haven't yet seen. The way to achieve this is by asking questions. Questions bring information to the surface.

You have to know how to ask questions, though. For example, "whys" can threaten people, so ask a lot of "whats."

Jesus was a Master at asking questions. The Bible records over

300 questions that he asked. He often answered a question with another question. He frequently used questions to set up the "spike" (the point he wanted to slam home).

Don't be afraid to ask God questions. He can handle them; remember, he's got all the answers!

Your Bible study insights will dramatically jump as you leverage the power of asking good questions. When you look at a passage, get into the habit of asking the Journalistic Questions (who, what, when, why, where, how). Doing so will take your mind into the territory of exploration, and new sights will come into focus!

Consider asking more questions in your daily life. Ask ones that begin with "What," and see how things go when you do!

Chapter 4
See: Observation

To see is to observe the passage, looking for things you never noticed before.

Open my eyes, that I may behold wondrous things out of your law.
--Psalm 119:18

IT'S SO EASY TO MISS WHAT'S AROUND YOU

In the South, we used the vivid expression, *If it were a snake, it would have bit me!* We'd say it when we were looking for something, and it happened to be under our noses. On the Appalachian Trail, I've had snakes slither under my legs several times. With the undergrowth next to the trail, I didn't see them coming. Perhaps I wasn't quick or observant enough. So I started to pay closer attention. After all, when serpents are around, you have to be alert.

Have you ever "misplaced" your cell phone, only to realize ten minutes later that it was in your hand all along? How often do we miss what is right there before us? Or see things but not absorb them? As Sherlock Holmes said, *Watson, you see, but you do not observe.* To observe means to perceive what is truly there.

I've heard people say the Bible seems like a black-and-white, impenetrable wall of words. Somehow, the mass of text prevents them from taking a closer look at the words and verses. For whatever reason, they're not prepared to do so. *The purpose of this chapter is not to judge you but to equip you to see more than you've been seeing.*

All of us overlook things regularly. Go into a room you've never been in, then leave. How much do you remember about what was in that room? Or, what are you oblivious to on your daily commute? Have someone else drive while you look around. What do you see for the first time? What if you made it a habit to observe three new things every time you drove the route? Because people habitually overlook things, I ask (when I lead meetings), *What have we missed? What questions have we not asked that we should have asked?*

DETERMINE TO SEE THE BIBLE TRULY

What have you missed as you've read the Bible? What would you discover if you developed your "seeing muscles" now? Each time you pick up the Bible, ask, *What is here that I have never seen before?* Always assume that there is more to see than you have been seeing. There's no greater key to better Bible understanding than that.

During this stage, you see what the passage says without reading into it. Just observe what's there. Try keeping a journal and writing down your observations, and once you have a good idea of what's happening in the text, you can move on to interpretation.

OBSERVING THE BIBLE

I'd wager that you've gotten into "the believer's rut." You emphasize the identical words and syllables and have the same assumptions and interpretations each time you look at a verse. If so, you may have missed so much of what is there.

When I lead groups through the *Awake from Bible Slumber* process, even the most experienced Christians will see things they've never noticed. To prove the point, I experiment with perhaps the most well-known Bible verse of all, one that most Christians have memorized: John 3:16. The participants don't realize it, but in their minds, they have already determined the entire meaning of the verse. They focus on certain words and emphasize them the same way every time.

Look at John 3:16 for a few minutes. Read it out loud several times. What words and concepts do you always emphasize (even if subconsciously) when you read the verse? What words do you tend to overlook each time? What would you glean if you emphasized those words this time? Say the verse out loud and change your intonation. Emphasize something new. How does that affect your understanding of what Jesus was saying?

HOW MANY OBSERVATIONS CAN YOU MAKE ON A VERSE?

I will never forget my first assignment at Dallas Theological Seminary. My professor was the highly respected Dr. Howard Hendricks. For years he had motivated the students at DTS to drill much deeper into the word.

Hendricks told us to take Acts 1:8 and make 25 observations on it.

Wow, I thought, this is going to be tough. I can get maybe 5-10, but that's it. He wants 25?!

I began the assignment, going quickly at first and then bogging down. I came back to class and turned it in. The next assignment

Hendricks gave us? Observe 25 more things! By that time, I thought he was insane. And, of course, when we turned in *that* assignment, we were given the next one: Make another 25 observations!

How in the world can you make 75 observations on this one verse, Acts 1:8? The answer: It's easy. It's hard if you are trying to base it upon your theological and biblical presuppositions. It's impossible if you are merely giving interpretations of the verse. You can take the verse and fabricate whatever principles you can, but your list won't be long. Or, it will be far afield of what the verse is saying. But, if you get granular and read out of it what is already there, you can do it.

Here's how: Pick a verse (any verse!) and read it. Now, observe. Let's make it simple: *I observe that the first word in the verse is* _____. *The second word is* _____. *The first letter is* __. *That letter comes before the following letter,* __. *The subject of the verse is* _____, *and the verb is (are?)* _____. *I observe that it mentions three geographical areas. I see two modifiers for the noun.* And so on. Approach it like this, and you'll soon have dozens of observations. Every verse can yield hundreds or even thousands of them.

This process might seem trivial, but it's not. You learn to observe, and you start to note details that matter. Learn to see better, and you'll begin to wonder, *Why did the speaker use this word instead of another? Which one does he emphasize here? What flavor comes out in the passage? What do I learn for my spiritual walk?*

TEST YOUR POWERS OF OBSERVATION

Hendricks gave us the "Nine Dots Exercise" to show how people stay in their mental boxes and fail to observe. Here's the exercise: Look at the nine dots below. See if you can touch each one by drawing only four lines and not lifting your pencil from the paper while you do.

When people first try this exercise, they say the solution is impossible. But you can solve it. See the end of the chapter for the answer!

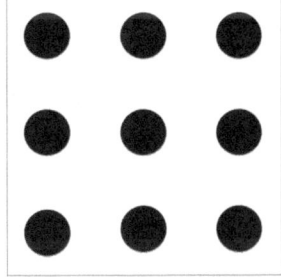

Can you connect the dots by drawing four lines without lifting your pencil from the paper?

A DEEPER DIVE

An Italian musician named Giovanni Maria Pala found that Leonardo da Vinci embedded a musical composition in his famous work, *The Last Supper*. Pala suspected that the painting had elements of a musical staff, and each hand of the disciples fit a musical note. But when he played the "tune," it didn't sound right. It dawned on Pala that Da Vinci liked to write backward, so Pala played the music backward. It worked! The tune was a dirge that evoked the moment of Jesus's betrayal pictured in the painting.

Artists frequently plant subtle symbolism in their works. In art and literature, there are nuggets of gold embedded for the one who observes. The same thing is true in the Bible.

We know that God built surprises into nature. He created living beings on the high mountain peaks and in the great depths of the ocean deep. God knew that few, if any, people would see them. But he did it because continual creative energy is a part of his being. He challenges us to explore that creation, even knowing

we'll only see a fraction. Our God is the Lord of Perpetual
Abundance.

God has also planted surprises in his word. For example,
scholars stumbled upon the idea of *chiastic* structure in literature
and began to notice it in Scripture. Chiastic comes from the Greek
letter chi, which looks like an X. It's a crossover form; a classic
example is, "When the going gets tough, the tough get going."
What is said at the beginning will be stated at the end. What is
said second will be mentioned next to last, and so on. Here are a
couple of short examples:

> *I do not sit with men of falsehood, nor do I consort with hypocrites.*
>> *I hate the assembly of evildoers, and I will not sit with the wicked.*
> —Psalm 26:4-5

> *Whoever exalts himself will be humbled, and whoever humbles himself will*
> *be exalted.*
> —Matthew 23:12

As scholars continued to observe, they learned that quite a few
passages have chiastic structures. You'll see chiasm in places such
as Genesis 6-9; Joshua 1:5-9; Psalm 1; Psalm 26:4; Psalm 90:1-2;
Isaiah 1:21-26; Joel 3:17-21; Matthew 23:12; and, Mark 2:27.
Chiasm is sprinkled through Romans also. If you want advanced
practice, then, observe the Bible for unique structural features.
Chiasm has always lurked in the Bible, just as diamonds exist
under the earth's surface. Similar to diamond mining, it took
digging to notice. Get below the surface with your Bible.

My point? We can always observe more. What surprises does
God have lurking for us?

NOW, LET'S PRACTICE SEEING!

Try this observation exercise: Close your eyes and think of what's in your room. What is the color of the curtains? How many lights are in the room? How many are on? Where is the furniture? What's on the desk or table?

Now, open your Bible and look at one tiny verse: John 11:35, *Jesus wept.* How many observations can you make on this, the Bible's shortest verse?

Next, let's go for a larger passage: Genesis 3:1-13. What do you see as you use the techniques described here? What insights do you receive (things you'd never noticed before)?

PARTING THOUGHTS

Get in the habit of intentionally seeing something different (new) each time you look at the passage. Don't fabricate something; see what's there! It's helpful to ask, *What have I not seen before?* Get out of "the believer's rut"! The more you look at the Scriptures, the more you will see. It all starts with "observation."

What are you missing (failing to observe) in your daily life? And what have you missed in the Bible? Practice observation to find out. Get in the habit of looking for new things in every situation.

As you do so, rather than ask, *What's wrong with the Bible that this is here?*, ask, *Why did God put this into his sacred word?* That one question will make a world of difference in your Bible insight.

THE SOLUTION TO THE NINE DOTS EXERCISE

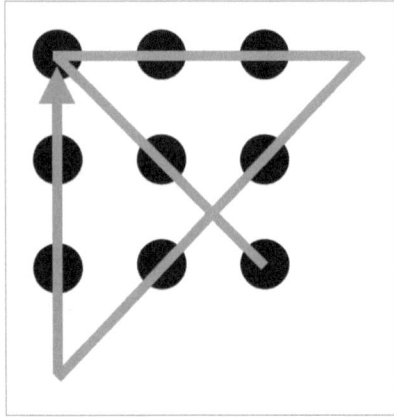

When people say this is impossible to solve, they make a grand, fatal assumption. They assume the lines must stay in the "box" of the nine dots. But you can connect all the dots by drawing a line beyond the box. Practice it until you get it.

The point, of course, is that we limit ourselves by our assumptions and hesitance to observe more deeply.

Part Three

Embrace the Power of Story

Chapter 5
Story: Drama, Narrative

*story is a dramatic or humorous narrative that interests or instructs.*

What's your favorite story?

People everywhere love stories. Stories grab our attention. They move us. They tell us about the human adventure. Ultimately, they talk about us.

For centuries the world's societies have had stories that explain and preserve their legacy. When you hear the story of another person, you understand his perspective. You see him differently. You might understand yourself better, also. Stories engage people's minds and motivate them. Everyone we run into has a story. And *you* have one!

Christians often underestimate how important stories are and how frequently they appear—even in the Bible! The Bible is story-saturated. Approximately 75% of God's word is story. Even the "non-story" parts, such as the Epistles (letters to churches), have a story behind them.

Paul's letter to the Romans is a good example. Why is it called Romans? Because Paul wrote it to the believers in Rome. It addresses their concerns and behaviors, touching on topics such as their relationship with the Lord, the association of the law to sin and grace, the relationship of Israel and the church, and how believers should handle disagreements over gray-area topics. The book is also quite personal; Paul salutes dozens of people in Rome at the end.

This chapter is here because understanding story is one of the premier tools for Bible insight. Once you grasp the story-related chapters in this book, it will forever enrich your Bible study. (Because stories are not limited by gender, and God works through all of us, I am intentionally alternating male and female in this book.)

WHAT MAKES A STORY?

Compelling stories have a purpose, a structure, and a flow. Structure comes in different forms, but in general, the design of a story is seen in this arc:

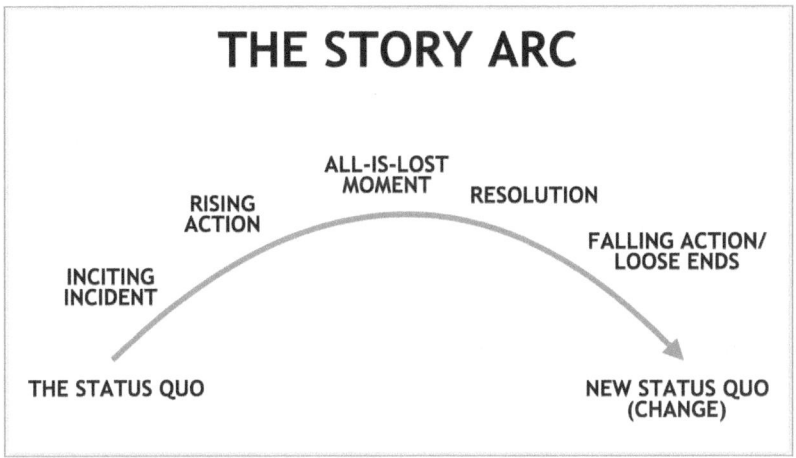

THE STORY ARC

STATUS QUO

The story usually begins with the hero (a.k.a. the protagonist) living everyday life. You could say that she is in a comfort zone. We call this section of the story exposition because it gives vital background. It tells the reader the stakes involved.

INCITING INCIDENT

Conflict enters her life. Some challenge pops up. It may come from an external force, or it may be internal, such as the hero's desire. The hero will have to resolve the conflict or achieve the desire. The most significant conflict in human history unfolds in the Garden of Eden, Genesis 3.

RISING ACTION

The hero has to leave his comfort zone to resolve the conflict. (Think *The Lord of the Rings*.) The hero has to go through unfamiliar/uncomfortable territory to do so. (Again, think *The Lord of the*

Rings!) The obstacles increase, and so does the tension. The story picks up momentum toward a confrontation.

The conflict takes a toll on the hero and may become overwhelming. He is tempted to pack it in. During rising action, therefore, the hero gets help from someone else. That person could be a mentor or colleague. Think Obi-Wan Kenobi mentoring Luke Skywalker. Athena (goddess of war, disguised as Mentor) mentoring Telemachus in Homer's *Odyssey*. Or Simon of Cyrene helping Jesus carry the cross.

ALL-IS-LOST MOMENT

A point comes in which the situation looks lost. The hero faces certain "doom," whatever doom means in the story's context. It's the hero's ultimate moment of conflict and change.

THE CLIMAX/RESOLUTION BEGINS

We reach the point of supreme tension. The hero confronts the enemy and resolves the conflict. She probably paid a price to resolve it, which might be heavy. It may be the hero's greatest moment of change.

FALLING ACTION

The story's momentum now heads toward a conclusion. The conflict has caused damage, and there are loose ends to clean up. What choices did the hero make during the climax? We'll find out their consequences now. Where will those choices lead the story? How has the hero changed?

As the tension subsides, falling action provides closure for the characters and the reader. And we must get the hero back home.

· · ·

NEW STATUS QUO/RESOLUTION ENDS

The story resolves, and the hero returns to his original, familiar setting. But, the hero is not the same; the experience has changed him. We see this story arc clearly in *The Lord of the Rings*. Or *Narnia*. Or *Titanic*.

But isn't new status quo also the story of Jesus Christ?

Even though you have rising action/falling action on both sides of the climax, the two sides are not equal in length. Typically, much more space is devoted to rising action because that's where the tension is. The audience is kept spellbound for a period of time. Falling action can be described more quickly.

I find that fascinating because it sheds light on the Bible's Story Arc. In the Bible, the rising action takes more time and space than the falling action. When you read the Bible through, you may be exhausted from the constant rebellion and judgment by the time you get to Malachi (the end of the OT). There are prophecies of restoration in each book, but the prophetic section may seem like a downer. By the end, the reader is almost desperate: *PLEASE, God, bring redemption! Get them and us out of this hopeless mess!* And God does precisely that in the upcoming Gospels.

NARRATIVE

A story becomes a *narrative* when events are told with purpose. A narrative has causes and effects. And it is related to point of view. Say you and your husband are telling your dating/engagement story. How you tell your friends may differ from what he says to his! Right? The same story happened, but you arranged things differently according to the context of the audience. (Not to mention what you both wanted for dramatic effect!)

Narrative happens when you choose what things to tell and in what order. A storyteller should strive to create a narrative that has impact. That doesn't mean that he makes things up. It means that he has to be selective. As the Apostle John said, the books of the world could not hold all that Jesus said and did, so the Gospel writers had to be choosy. They crafted their books under divine inspiration, but "handcraft" they did.

Near the end of his Gospel, John says, *These are written so that you may believe that Jesus is the Christ, the Son of God, and that by believing you may have life in his name* (John 20:31). No story is in the Bible by accident, and none are irrelevant. Each detail is there for a reason, even if it takes us some time to figure it out. Some 40 authors wrote the Bible over 1,500 years and could have included many more things. Each writer chose his narratives because of their special relationship to the point he was making.

Context makes all the difference in turning the story into narrative. Who is the audience, and what does it need to hear in the context? If Paul were writing 2 Corinthians to your church, would it be any different than the epistle he wrote to the Corinthians? I hope so!

You can rest assured that each story in the Bible was written for a purpose. If you can better grasp narrative styles, you will increase your insight into the Bible. Here are some of the types of narrative and some places we may see them in Scripture:

Descriptive: Descriptive narrative ties ideas and details together to convey time and place. It creates a mood.

Consider the unforgettable story of Jesus walking on the water, Matthew 14:22-33. The mood is subtly set in the previous story when Jesus withdraws in a boat to a "desolate place" by himself. After miraculously feeding thousands, he made the disciples go in a boat before him to the other side of the Sea of Galilee. Jesus dismissed the crowds and was alone. He went up a mountain by himself to pray. Aloneness is a persistent element in this story. As darkness descended, Jesus was "there alone," but the disciple-filled boat was in the midst of the lake, battered by a storm.

Alone without their leader and unsure about the situation, the disciples felt intense stress. (I can say from experience that when you are in a big storm on the water, without visible landmarks, your plans for the day mean nothing.) With this emotional condition intensifying their reactions, they were terrified when they saw the ghostly figure of Jesus walking toward them. They instinctively cried out in fear.

The Walking on Water story is not just about a miracle. It is an emotionally taut story that makes a subtle point about our relationship with the Lord Jesus. And about his relationship with God the Father. *What do we learn?*

Linear: Linear narrative coherently presents the story with a straight timeline. One event flows into another; *this happened, then that happened, then that happened.* We see things in the order they happened and the causes are evident. Much of the historical material in the OT flows this way; Exodus is a good example.

Nonlinear: In Nonlinear narrative, things are not presented in the order in which they happened. The timeframe moves around and may not seem as coherent as a straight timeline. Nonlinear is sometimes used to show a character's emotional state. When done well, nonlinear builds suspense vividly.

You're familiar with the most common version of timeline shift: Flashback. Flashback hooks the audience immediately and is very impactful. I chose to use it in my book on the Black Forest fire (*Nomad's Fire: Life at the Intersection of Loss and Significance*). Can you think of any flashbacks in the Bible?

The Psalms exude emotion, but they are not a linear story as a group. Most of them are free-standing. The contexts are not always given, but each psalm emerged from some situation in Israel's history. David wrote half of them. Psalm 51, for example, is his spiritual cry of repentance after committing adultery with Bathsheba and ordering her husband's execution as the cover-up.

Song of Solomon (a.k.a. Song of Songs) is a provocative study on several levels. It's not a narrative per se, but it springs out of the life of King Solomon. Scholars have tried to weave the narrative of its eight chapters together, but many attempts are forced and unsatisfying. One theory is that the book is a collection of individual songs; if that's true, it's not a romantic story arc after all.

Moving to the NT, something that may confuse you is that the Gospel writers vary the order of the stories. For example, Matthew, Mark, and Luke describe Jesus calming the storm differently. Each writer built his book around a theme and arranged his stories to develop it. That doesn't mean that the stories are fictional, though. By nature, all writing must be arranged in some fashion.

Quest: With Quest, the hero is on a journey toward a vital goal, and if he fails, the world may suffer disaster. The effort is all-consuming and will probably bring pain to the hero. There will be obstacles, arduous at times, and there will be a moment when all appears lost. In most cases, the hero will experience some trans-formation from the journey. We see all of these characteristics in *The Lord of the Rings*, but they are also vivid in the Bible.

The pattern of Quest narrative goes something like this: There is a (potential) hero. He is summoned to the journey. Helpers or mentors come to his side. (Frodo doesn't destroy the One Ring without the essential support from Samwise Gamgee.) The dramatic tension of Quest builds with significant challenges for the hero. From this, we get conflict, which gives us drama. The audience is pulled into the story, looking for the resolution. The conflict may be internal, external, or both. At a climactic point, the challenges threaten to bring certain destruction to the hero. But the hero survives, and the experience transforms him. The hero returns home, triumphant but changed.

Again, isn't this the story of Jesus Christ? He was triumphant but changed by the resurrection. And he experienced internal as well as external conflict. (In the Garden of Gethsemane, he asked God to take away the cup of suffering, but he did yield to God.) You could explore the internal and external journeys of Jesus Christ the rest of your days and never exhaust the pursuit.

Character Formation: With Character Formation narrative, you watch the protagonists grow and mature. They gain wisdom, experience, and humility. The experience will transform them. We see this moving pattern in books such as *To Kill a Mockingbird*, *Emma*, and the Harry Potter series. We see it in my favorite novel, Dickens' *David Copperfield*.

Many OT characters go through Character Formation. The book of 1 Samuel gives us two great examples: Samuel himself, and David.

The Character Formation of the disciples saturates the Gospels. Furthermore, Luke uses this narrative style for the human growth of Jesus himself in Luke 2: *And the child grew and became strong, filled with wisdom. And the favor of God was upon him* (v. 40); *And Jesus increased in wisdom and in stature and in favor with God and man* (v. 52). As God, Jesus required no growth. As man, he was conceived and born and had to grow in all respects.

. . .

Viewpoint: Viewpoint narrative presents the story from the point of view of a key character. We see the person's moods, emotions, beliefs, and values (right or wrong). Do you see this anywhere in the Bible? Although it's not a story per se, 2 Corinthians is a letter anchored to the experience of a rowdy church in a notorious Greek city. With strong emotion, the Apostle Paul addresses their attitudes and practices. (Those who denigrate the importance of emotion in the Christian life should revisit this book.)

Historical: We see how one thing causes another as the narrative progresses from historical event to event. Time passes, and there's cause, effect, and chain reaction. The Bible relies heavily on historical narrative.

There's a striking version of this in the OT book of Ezra. Although the book is in historical order, there is a large time gap between the book's first half and the second. The gap will confuse you until you look into the historical background. The Jews had been exiled. When it was time to return home, Zerubbabel returned with some of the people to rebuild the Jerusalem temple. That's Ezra 1-6. Some 60 years later, Ezra the priest and scribe returned. He led the people spiritually and had to call them to repentance. That's Ezra 7-10.

WHO'S THE PERSON?

We write stories in one of three "persons": First, Second, or Third. Why? Because the "person" gives the point of view or perspective, which is essential in telling the story.

First Person: The character (usually the protagonist) tells the story. He talks about himself, his opinions, and what happens to him. It's the "I/we" perspective. You see the story through his eyes. The reader becomes more attached to him. We don't see First Person as much in the Bible, but watch for it in Acts on those occasions when Luke says, "We." There's a legendary use of it in Genesis: *Let us make man in our image* (Genesis 1:26).

Second Person: The speaker speaks directly to another person or group ("you"). It's their point of view. We see Second Person in the "Epistles" (letters in the NT) because the writers wrote directly to churches and individuals. A classic example of Second Person is when Paul fusses out the Galatians, Galatians 3:1: *O foolish Galatians! Who has bewitched you? It was before your eyes that Jesus Christ was publicly portrayed as crucified.*

Third Person: An external narrator tells the story. The point of view is that of the person or people she talks about. She describes their actions and thoughts. The perspective is "he/she/it/they." The readers tend not to get as emotionally attached if the writing is in Third Person. Bible writers mostly use Third Person. They also use it when they speak of themselves. For example, the Apostle John described himself as *the disciple whom Jesus loved* instead of saying *I*. It's more indirect and humble.

THE BIBLE AS STORY

The Bible has a grand story arc. It is the ultimate narrative, written with intent and impact. It vividly tells of God's love for his creation and his self-sacrificial way of pulling humans out of their sinful predicament. All seems lost, but he saves them and eventually takes them to their "eternal comfort zone" as changed people.

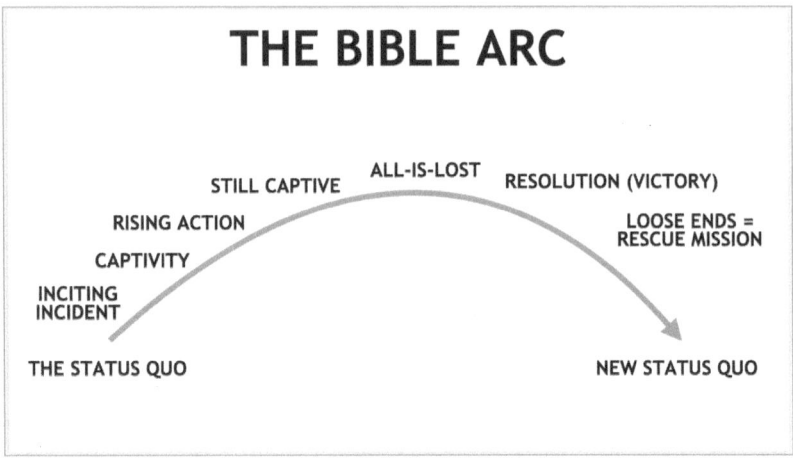

THE BIBLE ARC

The Bible books themselves are full of smaller stories and scenes. Each scene plays a part in a book's grand story (or theme or argument). Each scene can be dramatized somehow. When you look at a Bible story, ask yourself why God put the scene--and its details--into His sacred word.

The Bible comes alive when we see it as drama. At least three-fourths of the Bible is story, and the other one-fourth has story in the background. If Bible passages are stories, that makes them dramas with scenes and characters. Those characters have backgrounds that got them where they are. And there is your story.

Even the non-story passages ("non-narrative") have characters such as the author, God, etc. In other words, there is some circumstance behind the passage.

Your Bible study will come alive when you analyze a passage as a drama. Pretend you are watching the story acted out. The opportunities to observe and dramatize Bible passages are limitless!

As you do so, you will be asking questions such as:

- What is the context of the scene?
- Is there conflict in it?
- How does the scene progress?

- How does it transition from one thing to the next?
- What are the characters' motivations, and how do they get what they want?

STORIES IN THE OLD TESTAMENT

When I ask groups to give me a Bible story, the first one mentioned is usually David and Goliath (1 Samuel 17). I encourage you to tackle that one with a group. The segment of David and Goliath has all of the elements of story, including setting, characters, staging (location and positioning of the characters), conflict, action, dramatic steps, motivations, tactics of manipulation, dramatic tension, and resolution. See how interesting it gets when your group digs into the Story Arc and narrative details. And how fun does it get when they try to stage it?

STORIES IN THE NEW TESTAMENT

The Gospels are full of stories; you can jump in almost anywhere to see fascinating narrative details.

But what about the Epistles? They are letters, not narrative books. Is it impossible to dramatize them? To the contrary! Some creativity can make it happen! How would you bring Philemon to life? It's short and has a very distinct and relatable story background. It would make for an engaging and timely stage play.

Galatians is another example. In the region of Galatia (part of modern Turkiye/Turkey), the people had retreated in their faith. Paul fusses them out in the book, laying on them tremendous theology, practical exhortation, and acute conviction. Paul uses their situation to tell everyone what the fruit of the Spirit looks like, with a list of examples.

What if you took Galatians and had someone read it out loud, with dramatic intonation? Imagine the impact! And what if you took Galatians and converted it to scenes with dialogue and direct character interaction? The classic scene would be Paul chewing out Peter. Rest assured that you can adapt the book while keeping its integrity and inspiration intact if you stay aligned with its message.

A LIVELY EXAMPLE FOR PRACTICE

Take the story of Lazarus (John 11) and see what you can make out of it in terms of story.

- What is the "narrative arc" of the story?
- What are the little steps that move the story forward?
- How much emotion is experienced by the characters, and by whom?
- How is the audience changed by the end of the story?
- What impact does the story have on you?
- What impact did the experience have on Jesus?

PARTING THOUGHTS

A story is a narrative, either actual or fictitious, designed to interest, amuse, or instruct the reader or listener. Stories engage people's minds and motivate them. Stories have characters. Those characters have backgrounds that got them where they are.

The Bible itself is a grand story. Bible passages are usually stories. That makes them dramas with scenes. How does that affect how you see the Bible? And what does that tell us in terms of making it come alive? What if you thought through the dramatic angles of your passage? What could you do to make that particular story come alive with a group?

Even the non-story passages ("non-narrative") have characters, such as the author, God, community, etc. In other words, there is some circumstance behind the passage.

When you approach the Bible from the story perspective, you find that the opportunities to observe and develop Bible passages are limitless! Your Bible study will come alive when you analyze a passage as a drama. Pretend you are watching the story acted out (because you are).

Speaking of groups, if someone asks you to talk to a group, don't panic! Find a Bible passage, or see if they will assign one to you. Look at it with the suggestions in this book, study its dramatic angles, and make a spiritual point or two for your audience. Your message could be powerful!

Finally, be encouraged: *You never have to worry about a lack of material when speaking about the Bible!*

Chapter 6
Scene: Segment Of Story

scene is a story segment describing what happens between characters.

What is your favorite movie scene? Whatever it is, something about it jolts your nerve endings. And it's likely that the scene is an important part of the movie.

Stories are composed of scenes. A scene is a sequence of action and dialogue between characters. It happens in a particular place at a specific time. One of the characters is the focal character, and you'll see the story unfold from that person's point of view.

The scenes together form a continual series of bricks that build upon each other until the story is fully constructed. So the story is the overall unit, which is composed of scenes, which are composed of steps.

STORY >>> SCENE >>> STEPS

A scene is, therefore, a slice of the whole story. Without

scenes, there would be no play or movie; nothing would happen between the story's beginning and ending.

What is the reason for this scene in your story? How does this scene connect with the previous one? How does it lead to the next one?

Learn to observe how the writer builds the story and its scenes. It may seem accidental, but it is not, especially if it is a scene from Scripture. Whether the reader sees it or not, the writer is constructing an "argument" with the scenes.

In a story, action flows from one incident to another. There's a conflict experienced by the character and observed by the reader. In effect, you, the reader, are eavesdropping on the conflict. As the scenes develop, the character does not know how the story will end (unless he's Jesus!). And neither do you—although you'll try to guess!

A scene creates dramatic tension that moves the story forward to the next scene. When we watch mystery movies, we like to see unexpected plot twists that take the story in different directions. Do you realize the Bible itself builds plot tension and has twists of its own?

In reading the Old Testament this year, I noticed how the writers (especially Moses) built dramatic tension with their stories and gave the reader the punch lines at the end. A great example of dramatic tension is the story of the crossing of the Red Sea (Exodus 14).

The conflict that develops in front of us could be a physical altercation, a pointed conversation, a problem in the environment, or an internal wrestling within the character. The tension rises to a climax at the right pace and intensity. (For example, think of Jesus going to the Garden of Gethsemane and what happened there.) The scene should have a strong ending that perfectly matches the tension.

With a scene, you give the audience not an abstract summary but a description of the *exact thing* that happens between characters. The reader feels the conflict. The story comes alive. The writer does not have to give you directly all the information he wishes to convey. You learn it through the story rather than lecture. A narrator may fill in some information, but narration is less engaging than observing action between characters.

This is why the Bible is full of stories and scenes. God could have given us a giant lecture book, but he chose not to. He created us, so he knew better than to do that. God is a God of story, and he knows that stories grip us. And why they do.

A good writer pulls you into the scene by describing the conflict with sensory, concrete detail. Sensory means that he draws you into the mood. You'll read about sights, sounds, intonations, smells, tastes, and touches. Mark makes the story of the feeding of the 5,000 more vivid when he says that it took place on the green grass (Mark 6:39). The trick for the writer is to make the sensory experience fit with the situation and to have "just enough" detail; not too much, not too little.

Scenes generally move forward chronologically, but some books and movies mix the order. Even in the Bible, some passages, especially in the Gospels and Acts, are arranged according to theme rather than chronology. The purpose is what matters.

People and situations change during a scene and will somehow be different by the end of it. If there is no change, there's no need for the scene. Watch for transitions and notice the changes in time and location. Notice how a character transforms in attitude, behavior, emotions, and choices. In the scene, does she improve or worsen? A great example is the story of the Samaritan Woman, John 4. Read it closely and watch the woman's transformation.

Scenes may be short or long, but length isn't necessary for effectiveness. Generally, the longer the scene, the more critical it is to the narrative.

A scene usually has a beginning, middle, and end; it is a mini story arc. Watch how the action develops during it. You'll be better able to do this after reading the steps/narrative beats chapter.

Speaking of Moses in Exodus, what do you learn about him in the golden calf incident (Exodus 32)? Look at the passage closely, and you'll see that it was a remarkable display of Moses's spiritual priorities. Moses told God he did not want to replace Abraham as the "father of Israel." Moses passed the test with flying colors. (The Israelites did not.)

Exodus 3 gives us the classic scene of Moses walking by the burning bush. Was Moses the only character present? No, because God was also there, speaking out of the bush. God is a character. Watch how he enters and leaves the scenes he's in. He always does so when the time is right.

I've been encouraging you to read Scripture stories with fresh eyes. If you read a passage as if for the first time, you'd be better able to spot the dramatic tension. For example, consider the story of the "Rich Young Ruler" who encounters Jesus, Luke 18:18-30. Read it as if you don't know the spiritual choice he makes until the end of the scene. You'll feel a rising pity and regret for the young man. Subtly, Luke has you thinking about your own spiritual condition. *Have I valued my possessions more than my Lord?*

As far as the disciples went, the ultimate plot twist was the Resurrection. None of them saw the empty tomb coming. We eavesdrop on their excitement as they watch the unfolding of shock, doubt, surprise, and joy on the morning of the Resurrection.

In a scene, the characters cause actions or react to them. The scene may improve the lot of the main character or make his life worse. He may show a range of emotions. Or, he may not show emotion when you expect him to. The characters will probably speak to each other, and their speech will have distinct verbal intonation. You don't see their emotions in black and white; the writer either tells you, or you must intuit them. In Scripture, we must read closely to see the elements of emotion and behavior. It's not like a play or movie where we see body language portrayed in front of us.

The characters will move in some way. They may move in, out, toward, or away from each other. Stage left, stage right. On stage, off stage. Notice this little detail in the David and Goliath story (1 Samuel 17:48): While Goliath was being his blustery, oblivious self, David quickly advanced toward him. From a tactical perspective, the movement would have surprised Goliath. He would have paused. David quickly loaded the sling and fired. Goliath didn't have a chance.

Be sure to note which characters appear in which scene. The choice of characters is related to the author's purpose, and sometimes characters are introduced to foreshadow important appearances later. Luke does this frequently, such as with Stephen (Acts 6-7) and Saul (Acts 7-9).

A SPLENDID SCRIPTURE TO USE FOR EXPLORING SCENE

A chapter that I like to use for exploring scene elements is Matthew 8, which contains one story after another. They fascinate the reader by showing Jesus in action amid a universe of creatures (human and spirit) who react to Him and their circumstances.

Take Matthew 8 and observe some or all of the scenes. Which characteristics do the scenes display? If you're in a group setting, have people play the characters. Look for sensory imagery, intonation, emotion, conflict, and rising tension. How do the scenes lead from one to another?

A more advanced question about this passage is, *What purpose does Matthew have in expounding these scenes in this part of his book?*

PARTING THOUGHTS

A scene is a unit of action or a story segment in a play, movie, TV show, etc. It usually describes the things that happen between specific characters in one place.

A story will usually contain multiple scenes.

The scenes will have steps, also known as narrative beats. (We'll see more on that later.)

Always seek to understand the context of the scene.

There may be conflict in the scene. Is the conflict obvious or subtle?

Observe how the scene progresses. How does it transition from one thing to the next?

Always ask this vital question: *Of all the things that could have gone into the Bible, why did God put this scene—and its details—into his sacred word?*

There is great power in learning to identify the parts of a scene and how they affect the sweep of the biblical story. Learn to recognize the components. See how that deepens your understanding of the word and appreciation for our Sovereign God!

Chapter 7
Step: Narrative Beat

step is a bit of action or dialogue which moves the story ahead; it's a moment of change.

This chapter will give you a key to understanding a story's scenes and how to stage them.

THE BEAT MUST GO ON

A writer does not randomly throw together scenes. Each is composed of small steps, which are known as narrative beats. In theater and film, a beat is the smallest structural unit.

The beat is something that happens to move the plot forward. It may be subtle rather than a big event. It could be an action, a decision, a comment, or a revelation. Whatever it is, the beat intensifies the plot, accelerating it or sending it in a new direction. Scenes have multiple beats, one following another.

BIBLE BEATS

If stories and scenes have beats, we should expect to find them in the Bible. And we do. The sacred word contains thousands of them. You'll discover them when you look for the actions and steps that move the story forward.

For example, the beats are alive in the story of the raising of Lazarus from the dead (John 11). Here are some of them: Jesus came to Bethany (v. 17). Martha heard he was coming and came out to meet him. They had a dialogue, which did not move the action forward per se but contained beats of thought. Then Martha called Mary, who came to Jesus. Mary's words moved Jesus. The bystanders gave commentary. Jesus went to the tomb. There was dialogue. Then Jesus commanded Lazarus to come out of it. Lazarus came out. In the process, several characters— including Jesus—burst out with intense emotion. You, the reader, feel the emotion. How can you read that *Jesus wept* and not be moved by pathos or curiosity?

Do we realize that under the inspiration of the Holy Spirit, the writer thought it necessary to include every one of those beats and line them up in that order?

THOSE SHIFTY BEATS

Beats move the plot along toward a goal. Not all are action-based; a beat may come from relational interaction. The dialogue may contain a revelation that serves as a beat. Who can forget Darth Vader telling Luke Skywalker, *I am your father!* A classic biblical example is the private dialogue between Pontius Pilate and Jesus. The questions and responses bounce the plot forward. Eventually, even though he's a cynic, Pilate realizes that Jesus is not guilty.

It may help you to think of beats as the "shifts" in the story. Shifts happen when someone makes a significant realization that changes her attitude, behaviors, or goals. (Christian coaches tell us that our personal life shifts are beats.)

Narrative beats take the story in a negative or positive direction, depending upon where they are in the arc. As they head in a negative direction, they give off a tone of fear. As they move in a positive direction, they instill hope. The right combination of beats, with the right pacing, keeps tension in the scene. After a beat, you should sense that something significant has just happened.

The beat may signal a change in direction. It may contain an important plot point. (When you watch a murder mystery, the plot points come at you quickly and subtly. Will you catch them? Will you remember them? Can you process them while other action is going on?)

Beats evoke emotional reactions in the audience, even if they are subtle. They produce suspense. Dramatic tension increases and creates a noticeable change in one or more characters. Watch a *Lord of the Rings* movie, and you'll get your fill of narrative beats.

As you study a scene, see if you can spot the fulcrum. That's when things can go either way for the leading character. The fulcrum is the essential narrative beat in the scene.

AN EXAMPLE FOR PRACTICE

Take a Bible passage, such as a small story or half a chapter, and have your group identify the beats. A longer story to examine is John 4, the account of Jesus and the Samaritan Woman (a.k.a. the Woman at the Well). Assign one person to be Jesus, one to be the woman, at least one to represent the disciples, and one to be the narrator. Each person reads the dialogue of his or her character. Reenact one section at a time, and then stop and discuss where the beats were. What shifted? How did the beats advance the story?

PARTING THOUGHTS

A narrative beat is a short bit of action or dialogue that delivers a tiny moment of change and moves the story forward. Without beats, there is no scene.

A beat is the smallest unit of a story or scene.

The beats give you significant clues as to what is happening in the story. Practice spotting the beats in a TV show or movie. Where are they? What's the fulcrum (when things can go either way for the character)?

Get in the habit of looking for the beats in the Bible. You'll see how the divine story moves along. You'll have a better understanding of what is happening and why. Understanding narrative beats is a hidden key to Bible study!

Does the concept of beats apply to your own life? Of course it does! With that in mind,

- Can you identify the beats of God's will in your life?
- How and why did he line them up the way he did?

Chapter 8
Stars: Characters

S tars are the characters. Each has goals, emotions, behaviors, and life background.

WHAT A BUNCH OF CHARACTERS

This chapter will motivate you to look deeper into the Bible characters and equip yourself to dramatize their stories more effectively. While the story's message drives us, the characters bring the narrative to life.

Most of us can name our favorite movie or TV stars—the heroes, love interests, "second bananas," and villains. The actors animate the characters. You probably agree that Harrison Ford IS Indiana Jones and that Benedict Cumberbatch does a marvelous rendition of Sherlock Holmes.

You won't have much of a story without characters. They include the protagonist (hero or leading character), antagonist (the protagonist's adversary), and supporting cast.

The supporting cast is often quite interesting in its own right. "Second bananas" add spice, as they bolster the hero on her quest and bring punch to the story with their personalities. Does the Bible have any second bananas?

A cameo is when a recognizable person surprisingly pops up in a minor part of one scene. Do we have cameos in the Bible? Sure! How about in 1 Samuel 27:7ff, when Saul visits the Witch of Endor? They are shocked when the deceased prophet Samuel rises from the ground and appears before them.

Can you name your favorite Bible characters? Why are they your favorites? What do they do, say, or think? In your mind, what actors or actresses would best play them?

THOSE ROWDY BIBLE FOLK

How does this relate to Bible study? Simple. The Story Arc of the Bible covers thousands of years and involves thousands of named and unnamed characters. Without its characters, the Bible has no story arc. If you're going to go deeper in Bible study, you must dig into the analysis of the characters: *What role do they play in the story? What are their motivations? How do they encourage or sadden you? Do they inspire you? Repulse you?*

It starts with God as a "character" in his own right. Don't we want to study his role as thoroughly as we can? And how can we not examine the character and personality of a man like David? In the NT, what do we learn from the different personalities and backgrounds of the disciples?

If you have no beings, you have no stories. God created the world, but then he created characters to populate and tend that world. The story of the Creator and his characters illumine history and his work over thousands of years. The Bible is the narrative of God and His creatures—angelic, human, and animal.

Creation, innocence, paradise, fall into sin, turmoil, redemption, heaven, hell. In the wild narrative arc of the universe are billions (trillions?) of individual stories played out.

PRACTICING BIBLE CHARACTERIZATION

Dramatizing the characters is a potent group activity. It works well for a class or Bible study. It also creates a fantastic retreat experience.

You can choose Scriptures from all over the Bible, but I highly recommend starting with Genesis 3. You will see insights from this passage that had never occurred to you before.

To make it a group activity, assign people the roles in Genesis 3 and give them time to study their characters in light of the whole chapter. Then dramatize the story in front of the group. Choose a narrator who reads (with intonation!) everything except the dialogue. The "actors" perform the dialogue based on how they perceive their characters (emotions, motivations, personalities, etc.). What is each character's motive in the scene? There are usually multiple motivations; we rarely understand everything going on (see Job's friends as an example!).

What are the characters facing internally and externally? Their body language and intonation should match the dialogue. The actors will use actions, words, and expressions to tell the audience who the character is and what he or she seeks. The chapter will come alive in front of you.

If you are studying the Bible independently (and not in a group), you must bring the characters to life in your mind if you want to see the Bible itself come to life. Make at least three observations on each person: Personality, style, body language, facial expression, motivations, etc. And what about fashion? (Even Adam and Eve had to get dressed!)

No matter which way you're doing it, observe the characters closely, and look for insights such as these:

- What is the character's goal in the scene? (This is an excellent question for understanding. You don't grasp the story until you get a decent grip on the motivations.)

- Is the character facing any obstacles?
- What is the background of the character? What does your intuition tell you about her upbringing?
- What emotions does the character display? (There's probably more than one.)
- How does the character scheme to get what she wants?
- How does the character expect the scene or story to conclude?
- What does the character do with her body? (To make a story come alive, envision the characters' body language.)
- Is there a conflict with an antagonist? The introduction of conflict captures our interest. It is usually between two humans, but it may be between the character and God (the book of Job), the character and Satan (Jesus and the temptation), the character and angels (either good angels or demons), the character and animals (Jonah and the whale, Balaam and the donkey), or the character and nature (Peter and the Sea of Galilee, Elijah and the tempest on Mount Horeb).

CHARACTER-STAGING TECHNIQUES

If you reenact a Bible story with a group, the following character-staging techniques will help everyone bring the characters to life:

- Blocking: How is his body positioned on the stage in relation to the other characters? What does that tell you about their relationship? Closeness? Distance? Fear? Hostility?
- Movement: Does the character move in the scene? How? How quickly? Why? What does that indicate

about his motivations, thoughts, and emotions? Is he greedy? Afraid?

- Inflection: How does she emphasize her lines? What is her tone of voice? What does that reveal about her thoughts, emotions, and goals? Is she trying to manipulate others? Is she articulate? Does she sound intelligent? Does she slur her words?
- Projection: Does he speak loudly or softly? How does that relate to the purpose of the scene?
- Facial expressions: Which does she use? How do her expressions show reactions and emotions?
- Body Language (non-verbal): What is his body doing? What does that reveal about his emotions and spiritual motivations? Are his non-verbals consistent with what he's saying?
- Listening: Does she listen to the other characters? How? What is her body language? What does that tell you about her heart and her desires?

SOME MORE TIPS FOR PLAYING THE ROLES

This list will help you develop your understanding of the scene and its characterization:

- Who spoke? Where were they?
- Why did they say it?
- Whom did the speaker care about the most? (Himself? The hearer? God? Someone else?)
- Whom did they say it to?
- Was the hearer hostile or friendly?
- What authority did the speaker have to say what she said?
- Was the speaker being honest? (Can we trust all the speakers in the Bible? Heavens, no!)

- Was the speaker serious, pensive, joking, angry, happy, or afraid?

This analysis forces you to consider a person's motivations, emotions, expressions, and appearance. It engages you more deeply in the biblical drama. And it gives you substantial raw material for application!

Technology may have changed dramatically over the centuries, but human emotion remains the same. How would you have reacted to the situation the character faced?

In exploring the scene and watching what happened to the character, how can you learn and improve yourself? Did you spot any weaknesses that you share? Would you have chosen the path she chose? What would have happened to you? What do you learn from both the character's positive choices and her mistakes? The potential is endless.

And don't miss the humor in character interactions. Think of Rhoda, Peter, and the oblivious Jerusalem church in Acts 12. The interaction between Balaam and his donkey (Numbers 22) is a classic drama with a dose of slapstick. (The larger story of Balaam, though, is tragic and violent.)

MAKING BIBLE MOVIES—OR YOUR CHURCH PASSION PLAY

Producers face a major challenge when they film the Bible. The viewers have preconceived notions about the characters: Looks, personality, behavior, etc. Whom do the producers cast for the roles? And all Bible characters except for one will be sinners. How should they be played?

And, of course, the most demanding role to cast and play is that of Jesus. Reenacting him is a sobering and humbling experience, not to mention that everyone has perceptions about his looks and style. If you think that the actor playing Jesus will get the "big head," I can tell you from experience that the opposite is probably true. When a small child looks up at you and thinks you are Jesus, you'll have a responsibility on your shoulders as long as you live in town!

To a smaller degree, we face characterization questions when we produce church Passion Plays. It takes effort to get the look and the behavioral balance "just so." The audience will be more forgiving, though.

PARTING THOUGHTS

You can't study the Bible well without exploring the characters. So answer these questions, and your Bible study will be more gold than Oscar's:

What are the characters' goals (motivations) in the scene?

What obstacles does the hero face?

What emotions do the characters display? (Look for more than one each.)

What tactics or schemes does the character use to get what he wants?

How does the character expect the scene or story to conclude?

What does the character do with her body? Some considerations:

- Blocking: how is her body positioned on the stage in relation to the other characters?
- Inflection: how does she emphasize her lines?
- Projection: does she speak loudly or softly?
- Expressions: what facial expressions does she use?
- Body language: what is her body doing?
- Listening: How does she listen to the other characters? (A listening character helps to bring focus and passion to the scene.)

Please don't forget: The biblical characters were not unapproachable superheroes. They were real flesh and blood people, no different than you. We see ourselves in them, and they are relatable to us. Peter was similar to the guy you go fishing with. Esther would have gone to the coffee shop with you and been your best friend forever. We commit the same sins, have the same fears, and enjoy the same hopes. So play your characters like the real people they were. (People gravitate to *The Chosen* because the characters come across as genuine rather than cardboard stereotypes. We can relate to them.)

Closing questions for your life:

- Your own life is a character arc. How would someone play your character? Which emotions and expressions would he or she emphasize? What's the body language?
- Which actor would fit you the best, and why?

Chapter 9
Staging: Placement, Movement

S taging is the placement and movement of characters in the scene.

If you had to put the Adam and Eve story on stage, how would you do it? Would you place them together? Is Adam on stage the whole time? Where does the serpent come from, and how does he position himself? Does he leave? Where is God? Does he move in and out, or is he lurking the whole time?

This chapter is about what we can glean from the Bible stories by thinking about how to stage them.

STEP UP TO THE STAGE

Every story has a setting and location. Bible stories have grand locations (such as Israel), but they also have "ground" locations. Stories are grounded in specific places. A historic well in Samaria. A threshing floor. A field in the Valley of Elah. A cross at Golgotha. Our Bible stories are grounded to locations; even heaven is described as a place!

The setting, or context, includes the grand and the ground locations. But staging is about the ground location and how we bring it to life in front of us. To reenact the Adam and Eve story, for example, we have to visualize how they moved and placed themselves in the Garden of Eden. To figure that out causes us to look more closely at the Bible's details. Open Genesis 3 and read the tale of the serpent, Eve, and Adam in the Garden.

- Where would you place each of them in the scene if you had to stage it?
- Does the serpent approach Eve, or does she approach it/him?
- Where is Adam when this happens? Does he come on the scene? If so, how and from what direction?
- Is Adam there all along? Is he lurking?

(I'll give you a secret: No matter what you do with Adam in this story, he doesn't come out well!)

WHY TALK ABOUT STAGING?

What is a stage? It's the platform on which we enact the drama/story.

Staging in Bible study is imagining what the setting looked like, how large or small it was, how it was "decorated," how the characters in the story positioned themselves, and how they moved. Did they move alone? Together? Counter to each other? Toward each other? On or off the stage?

When you study the Bible, you probably visualize these things without realizing it. When you dramatize them with a group, you'll have to look at your setting and decide the best way to stage the story with the features and limitations of your location. Any story or Bible passage with dramatic dialogue should include relevant staging. You cannot bring to life a scene unless you imagine what its staging and movement should be.

ON- OR OFF-BROADWAY

A playwright develops a stage play knowing that the producers and director must adapt the script to a theater stage. Stages vary in dimension, but all of them have limits. Extraordinary creativity has to go into designing and building the sets. It's not only about the look; it's about how the stage will function in tandem with the action and dialogue.

A theater separates the stage from the audience by a frame called the proscenium, which subtly suggests to the audience that they are eavesdroppers peering into the lives of strangers. The theory is that the audience watches the characters with an invisible wall between them. Only rarely do the actors "pierce the veil" and look and speak directly to the crowd.

In movies, the proscenium is the camera. The actors and audiences never see each other. As with theater staging, only rarely may an actor "pierce the veil" and stare directly at the camera. Ninety-nine percent of the time, the camera is an eavesdropper.

When we read the Bible, we eavesdrop on the stories. God wants us to observe and learn from what we see. That's why he brought the Bible into being.

The smash musical *Les Miserables* was known for years for its revolving stage. The musical used a turntable stage that rotated over seventy times during the play. Actors had to move on and off the turntable with precise timing. *Phantom of the Opera* is a legendary example of staging. In addition to the falling chandelier, the musical has a luscious scene in which the Phantom and Christine glide across the stage in a boat. The director uses lighting and fog to disguise the mechanical parts. The staging of a Broadway musical is complex and frantic behind the scenes.

Whether stage play or movie, the director has to take the script and think of the most engaging and effective ways to portray the scenes. How are the characters positioned on stage? How do they act and react? How do they move individually and together? How are the narrative beats expressed? Most importantly, how does all of that effectively portray the plot? After all, the event is not about technology or sumptuous staging; it's about a compelling story and characterization.

In other words, the directors must decide how to "stage" the stories. How do we apply that to Bible study?

STAGING THE BIBLE STORIES

Address the following details if you're dramatizing a Bible story on stage, such as during a worship service. You'll have limits on your stage dimensions, set decorations, and available time, but you can still produce something powerful.

You can forego many of these items if you're dramatizing the Bible story with a group (and not for an audience). Your primary purpose is to understand the Bible much more deeply. So focus on the story's purpose, accurately-portrayed dialogue, and the behavior and motions of the characters. That includes non-verbal communication.

Whether you perform the story on an actual stage or reenact it with a private group, you'll need to know some basic information about staging. Here's a list of things to consider, all based on the story and its progression of plot:

- How do the characters stand in relation to each other? "Blocking" is the theater name for the positioning of a person on stage in relation to the other characters. So, how will you block the actors? Going back to Genesis 3, you'll have to think carefully about the positioning of Adam and Satan. Was Adam present when Satan tempted Eve? What was the body placement and language? Positioning forces you to go to the Bible and study it closely. In so doing, you'll gain insights into the relationships between the characters. See the options below.

- What's the body language of the characters?
- What are their non-verbal expressions?
- Is there movement during the scene? In what direction(s)? How do characters enter and exit the stage? If a character moves toward another character, it could be a movement of hostility or attraction. Is the narrative beat of the scene moving in a positive or a negative direction? (For example, the woman with the issue of blood in Luke 8:43ff moved toward Jesus, touched his garment, moved away, and then fell before him.) Judas Iscariot in the Garden of Gethsemane moved toward Jesus, kissed him, and stepped back. The soldiers came toward Jesus. The disciples ran away.
- If it's a drama on stage, you'll need marks or numbers on the platform to help the characters know where to stand.

NOW, TURN UP THE HOUSE LIGHTS AND PRACTICE STAGING

Pick a few juicy Bible passages and think about how you would stage them. Plan the staging by sketching them on graph paper or a small whiteboard. (This is a mini-version of "storyboarding," which is when a director has someone produce a series of sketches to show the narrative movement of the movie. He storyboards in advance to ensure everything makes sense, to help the crew prepare for the film, and to save production costs.)

Stage managers use diagrams of the stage, correct to all dimensions. Have some blank sheets which contain the stage boundaries in proportion to the actual measurements. Plan your sets, props, and character movements on the stage templates. If you have several unclear choices regarding the scene, try sketching them.

While this is important for stage productions, the process also works for group study. Show the stage template on a whiteboard. Designate one person to be the "artist." Have the group read the passage together and determine where to place the characters on the template. Upon finishing the scene, photograph the whiteboard so you don't lose your work. How would you sketch the Garden of Eden incident (Genesis 3)? The miracles of Jesus?

Another idea is to use a tabletop and choose random items to represent the characters and set pieces. Use chess pieces, Lego characters, ketchup bottles, or whatever you have on hand. Use a marker board with magnetic holders.

Anyone can practice staging. It is a marvelous thing to do with children and teenagers. Everyone loves a good story, and you won't beat the Bible's stories. Have the kids help you set up the staging. Be creative. Be sure to ask the kids how they would position each character.

Doing all of this forces you to study the passage. And yet, the study won't feel "academic." Everyone will own the desire to learn and to portray it effectively.

You have hundreds of staging choices from the Bible. One great option is to bring to life the Joseph story. His brothers had once sold him into slavery. Years later, they came before him when he was a high official in Egypt. How did they react when he revealed himself to them (Genesis 45)? No words must be said to portray the story; staging and acting can carry the day.

How would you stage the Last Supper? (Hint: It's not how

Leonardo da Vinci painted it!) You would have to read each Gospel and see what happened. Who was involved, how were they positioned, and how did they belly up to the table(s)?

PARTING THOUGHTS

As you read Scripture, think about how to place the characters in the scene. Where do they stand? How close are they to each other? How do they face each other?

Are they moving in the scene? How are they moving? (On the stage, off the stage, laterally, in or out, etc.?) What is their speed, direction, and behavior? As you get a grip on the concept of staging, your Bible study—and understanding—will never be the same.

Staging also applies to life itself. Wise people observe how others place themselves. How do they move? How do they position themselves in relation to others? What's the body language?

You're not "curtains" yet, so consider these questions from your own life:

- How has God staged you, and what characters does he bring onto your stage?
- Whom does he move into your life?
- Whom does he move out?

Part Four

Spot these Specifics

Chapter 10
Specks: Details

T o focus on specks is to notice the details of the structure (starting with the verbs).

For Ezra had set his heart to study the Law of the LORD, and to do it and to teach his statutes and rules in Israel.
—Ezra 7:10

Are you a "detail person"?

Many people say they are not! How many of our fellow citizens loved English in high school? But when people get into Bible study, they change. Why? Because it makes a difference when they realize that God built his word with bricks of detail and that the more they observed the little things, the more they saw the mind and heart of their Lord.

A speck is a particle, a small detail. Focusing on detail is paying attention to the individual, tiny parts of the material. This chapter will explore what it means to consider the bits of a Bible verse.

Do details matter in relationships? If your spouse were to tell you, "I love you, but...," upon what word would you fixate?! The little three-letter word "but," of course! That's all you would hear. A Valentines Day card may only cost a few dollars, but imagine if your loved one was expecting a card and you never gave it.

Details matter in culture. Popular movies leverage detail to great effect. The powerful movie *1917* was carried along subtly by the use of trees in the scenes. Did you notice? If you saw *Inception*, you learned to watch the spinning top. Sharp-eyed *Lord of the Rings* fans noticed that the ring melted on Mount Doom only when Frodo chose to be rescued by Sam. It was a departure from the book, but that little detail made a statement.

THE POWER OF THE ITTY-BITTY SPECKS

Details are essential to Bible study. The Bible is a massive collection of bits that mattered enough to God that he wanted to hand them down to you. Hebrews 4:12 says, *For the word of God is living and active, sharper than any two-edged sword, piercing to the division of soul and of spirit, of joints and of marrow, and discerning the thoughts and intentions of the heart.*

If what God says is living and essential, won't the Holy Spirit prompt us to care for the specks?

The Bible is a bounteous gold mine; the more you dig, the more you'll find. Here's one classic example: It makes a difference whether you use the definite article ("the") or an indefinite article ("a"). It is the difference between saying that Jesus is the Savior or only "a" Savior.

Furthermore, all sorts of details are essential. What verb tense does a writer use: Past, present, future, perfect, imperfect, etc.? What about the connective words? (and, therefore, because, etc.). Do these things affect God's message to us? Do they tell us something about theology? Yes. Because without them, we'd have no word from God and no theology.

Let's take the details of the word of God seriously.

DETAILS IN A SENTENCE—OR A VERSE

The chart below shows the parts of a typical sentence. Use this as a prompt when you look at a verse of Scripture. Charting a verse like this is a great way to understand what the author is saying, especially if the verse is long or confusing. (This is a basic form of sentence diagramming.)

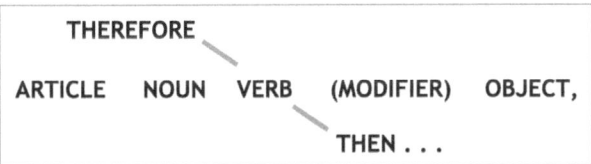

Your starting point should be the verb(s) of the sentence. The verb is the engine of the sentence. A verb is an action word ("hit" or "run," for instance) or a word of existence ("is," "was," "be," etc.). Verbs of existence describe a state that the subject was in, is in, or will be in, but they don't move the action forward on their own. Action verbs move things forward. So, what verbs are in your verse? What are they driving toward?

Who or what is the subject of the verse? The subject is the person or thing who is either doing the action or being described. For example, in *Jane hit the ball*, Jane is making the action happen. In *Jane is kind*, Jane is being described. The subject is usually placed first and tells us what the sentence is about or who or what performed the action. The short verse *Jesus wept* (John 11:35) tells us that Jesus cried at the death of Lazarus. The grammar is simple, but the concept is profound. (As you know from English class, the grammar can get more complex. But let's leave it there for now!)

What is the object of the verb? (In other words, what does the verb "act upon"? In the example above, Jane acted upon the ball.)

How are things described (in other words, "modified")? Mark tells us that the grass was green when Jesus fed the 5,000.

When did the event happen (verb tense)?

What words lead into the verse? If you find "for" or "therefore" early in the verse, then be sure to look at the previous verse(s) to see how this verse continues the discussion. "For" often means the reason or purpose.

"Then" tells you what happens next; it's what the statement leads into. The verse may cause it.

Get in the habit of looking closely at these types of details in a Bible verse.

SEARCHING FOR SPECKS: OTHER THINGS TO NOTICE

In addition to what we said about the parts of a sentence, look for these details:

- Are words or ideas repeated? That probably means the writer is emphasizing them, so take note.
- Do the verb tenses change in the sentence? Do the pronouns change?
- Is the command given to "you" singular or "you" plural ("y'all")? The Greek tells us, and perhaps your study Bible gives that information.
- Does the writer give details about the time or location?
- Is there a list of things, such as the *fruit of the Spirit* in Galatians 5:22-23?
- Does the verse seem to be related to what came before (which is what usually happens when you see "therefore," "for," "since," "because," etc.)? If so, what is the relationship between your verse and what came before? Did one cause the other?
- Is there an "if/then" relationship (if this, then that)?
- Does the verse contain a question or a statement?

- Does the verse seem to have emotion?
- Does it emphasize something?

LET'S SPOT SOME BIBLE SPECKS

You can do this on your own or discuss it in a group. With a group, you'll collect more observations.

You can practice this on almost any verse, but let's go for the gusto. Look up Romans 8:31-39 in your Bible and see what details you can observe. If you're doing this alone and don't have time to analyze all nine verses, try verses 31 through 33. Consider assigning certain verses to specific individuals if you're doing the exercise with a group.

What do you see? How do these details deepen your understanding of God?

SPECCING SOME HELPS

This chapter is an overview, but I pray it lights a fire in you to go even deeper. If it does, consider looking into an inductive Bible study course. They may meet locally or online. Here are some well-respected choices; I've included their web addresses for your benefit:

- Bible Study Fellowship, www.bsfinternational.org
- Community Bible Study, www.communitybiblestudy.org
- Precept, www.precept.org

PARTING THOUGHTS

Details add flavor and significance to your passage. The tiny ones can be crucial. For example, whether Jesus is "the" God or "a" God makes all the difference in the world.

When you look at the details, look for things like these:

- The verbs (action verbs and verbs of existence).
- Modifiers (things that describe or give color).
- Things that connect (such as "therefore").
- The itty-bitty words (such as "the" versus "a").

It will help you see how the parts fit together if you chart (diagram) your verse.

To get past the wall of words, look more closely at the bricks in the wall! You will discover many details once you start searching. Note the ones that seem especially important.

Before we leave the study of detail, ponder these questions:

- Of the many things that Jesus did on Earth, why did the writers select their chosen stories?
- Why were the details in your verse placed there?

They're not in the verse by accident.

Chapter 11
Site: Location

*S*ite is where the story takes place and what makes the location *significant.*

Have you been asked any of these questions lately?

- Where are you from?
- Where do you live now?
- Where are you going?
- What do you call home?

These are questions we use to "place" ourselves, to give us an anchor. As we've become a highly mobile society, these questions have gotten complicated. Where is home, for example, to a child of the military? Because of my nomadic life, I finally started answering the question with, *I'm from the Air Force.* That simplifies it. Military people know what I mean. I have no hometown.

You may not know your hometown, but at any given time, you have a location! You occupy some little spot on Planet Earth!

LOCATION, LOCATION, LOCATION

Imagine what your favorite movies would be like, without locations. They wouldn't exist. That's the case whether the movie is *Gone With the Wind*, *The Lord of the Rings*, *Titanic*, *Star Wars*, or *Pride and Prejudice*. All interweave with their locations. There might be a Little House, but it wouldn't be on the prairie!

God did not create a universe of clouds and marshmallows. He gave us soil to dig in, metal for tools, and Hatch green chile for our bellies (amen!). God created a physical world. He made us tactile, able to touch and feel his creation. And we are limited, bolted to the earth by gravity. We live in real, material places. We occupy one spot at a time in our bodies. The Bible even describes heaven itself in physical terms. It has trees, water, jewels, and gold (Revelation 21-22). It's a place that our senses will be able to experience!

The significance of location is often under-appreciated in Bible study. Location anchors a passage and even the Bible itself. It's where the characters are, where they've been, and maybe where they're going. It's impossible to fathom what your life would be if locations didn't exist. Now imagine the Bible without them. You can't! Be alert, therefore, to the significance of biblical location.

Site refers to the geographical locations in the Bible where the stories occur. But it also refers to how the characters move across the landscape. Site is similar to stage, but on a grander scale; it's the terrain on the earth on which the biblical characters lived and moved.

Great stories are often "odysseys," describing a character's long journey through vast terrain, thrilling places, and exciting experiences. The hero navigates significant obstacles along the way. He has dramatic experiences in—and because of—the location.

Many classic works are odysseys: The original *Odyssey* itself, by the Greek poet Homer; the various stories of Lewis and Clark, *The Lord of the Rings, Band of Brothers, The Last of the Mohicans, Huckleberry Finn, The Chronicles of Narnia, Moby Dick,* and *David Copperfield*. And *Star Wars*, of course. All of them have plots carried along by location.

Even if a story is not primarily a geographic odyssey, it may be an odyssey of mind, emotion, or character development. It may be a drawn-out character study. It may be one of relationship (perhaps tied to history and geography), such as in *Gone With the Wind*. Jane Austen wrote about odysseys of the heart.

The Bible itself is a spiritual odyssey over the landscape of the soul. In it, we see the choices and fate of humanity. It is the journey of God's people. The history of the church itself is an odyssey.

How many odysseys do you see in the Bible? Can you name them? A big one is the whole Bible itself, which is the odyssey of creatures returning to the Creator as he draws and saves them. But there are multiple smaller odysseys, such as the life of David; the transformation of Peter; the story of Israel; the life of Christ; and the growth of the church.

LOCATION AND THE BIBLE

How does this relate to your Bible study? To understand the Bible, you have to understand its basic geography. Most Bible books speak of location and movement. Have you ever considered how often the Bible characters are on the move? To take location out of the Bible would be to gut its significance.

Consider the flow of salvation history, as mentioned in the sections below. The story of salvation is, in part, a message of movement.

In the Bible, a location is almost always significant. It carries overtones of God's design and our response. The name of a place has meaning. What is spiritually significant about it? What does that tell you about the spiritual condition of those who live there, move there, or leave there? (The story of Lot's wife is a classic example. What does her desire to cling to a place of depravity say about her?)

Sometimes the location gives you some spicy flavor for the story. For example, consider Jesus' question to the disciples at Caesarea Philippi in northern Israel, a place of beautiful rock. Jesus asked, *Who do people say that the Son of Man is?* Peter answered: *You are the Christ, the Son of the living God.* Jesus responded, *[Y]ou are Peter, and on this rock I will build my church.*

Even if you're not a map person, see if you can get into maps for the sake of your Bible study. Grab a Bible atlas, a Bible dictionary, or a Bible encyclopedia to help you discover more about what makes the place significant.

You'll notice that rivers, seas, and mountains play critical roles. You're familiar with Mount Sinai, Mount Carmel, the Mount of Transfiguration, and the Mount of Olives, from which Jesus ascended and to which he will return. You know about Mount Megiddo but probably call it "Armageddon" (The Hebrew *Har Megiddo* is Mount Megiddo).

The rivers pop up frequently and help anchor the stories to the general locations and the events going on at the time. You know several rivers by heart: Jordan, Nile, Tigris, and Euphrates. (The Euphrates has significance in literal and metaphoric ways. It's related to Babylon, symbolically a place of rebellion against God.) You'll also encounter the Jabbok, Yarmuk, Arnon, and others. The famous seas of the Bible include the Sea of Galilee, the Red Sea, the Dead Sea, and the Mediterranean Sea. (Red, Dead, and Med!)

Ancient history in the biblical region tells us about the movement of empires to conquer their enemies and gain new territory. We read about Assyrians, Babylonians, Persians, Greeks, and Romans. The Bible narratives play out on a global stage.

LOCATION IN THE OLD TESTAMENT

Below is a basic map of the ancient region. Is it a coincidence that Israel, even though small in size, is the land bridge between three major continents?

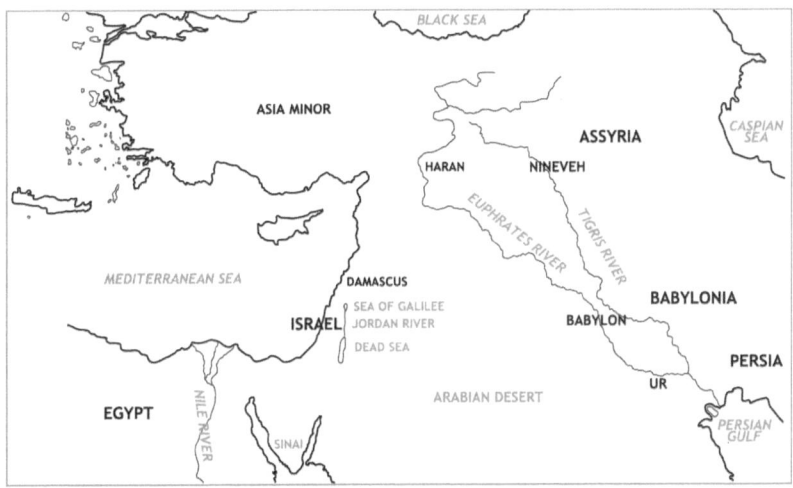

How important is location in the Old Testament? Look at this small sampling:

- Genesis 1-2: God creates the physical universe and places two humans in a named garden (Eden).
- Genesis 3: God removes Adam and Eve from the garden so that they will not eat from a specific tree (the Tree of Life) rooted in the garden.

- Genesis 10: The Tower of Babel (in Babylonia) and the spreading of the nations by confusing their languages. The Table of Nations follows.
- Genesis 12: Abraham is called from Ur of the Chaldeans (near the mouth of the Euphrates) to be the father of Israel and the nations.
- Abraham moves from Ur to Palestine, traveling along the Euphrates River.
- Joseph and Jacob's family go to Egypt.
- Moses leads the nation back, splitting the Red Sea and receiving the Law at Mount Sinai. Israel rebels at Kadesh Barnea and wanders in the wilderness for 40 years.
- Joshua leads Israel across the Jordan River and into the Promised Land.
- David runs from Saul in the desert, moves to the Philistine areas, and captures Jerusalem. It becomes the capital city of the kingdom.
- The nation of Israel divides into two Kingdoms, the Northern (a.k.a. Israel) and the Southern (a.k.a. Judah). The Divided Kingdom is the period during which the prophets ministered.
- Israel is taken captive to Assyria in 722 BC and never returns.
- Judah is exiled to Babylonia in 586 BC; God tells her to bless her "host" nation.
- The Persians conquer the Babylonians and assume control of the Jews in exile.
- Esther becomes Queen of the Persian Empire in the capital city of Susa.
- The Persians urge Judah to return from exile in 539 BC. The OT ends around 430 BC with Judah back home in the Promised Land, freshly chastened.

. . .

LOCATION BETWEEN THE TESTAMENTS

There is a gap of approximately 400 years between the OT and the NT. At the dawn of the NT, Judah is back home in the Promised Land, but there has been a major shift in world powers. (The chapter on the Story Arc of the Bible explains this.) The Roman Empire now controls the land. We did not see Rome in the OT. At the end of the intertestamental period, God sent his Son Jesus. Galatians 4:4 tells us he entered the world *in the fullness of time*. God's plan was precise as to not only the time but the location. Jesus was born in a hamlet named Bethlehem because he descended from King David. Micah 5:2 predicted that this would be the location.

THE NEW TESTAMENT

The New Testament is location-saturated. It begins with the domination of Israel by the Romans. The desire for freedom created an electric environment in Israel, as people were desperate for their Messiah to come and vanquish this despised foreign power. For hundreds of years, other empires had controlled Israel. The tense interplay between Rome and Israel is the backdrop to the Gospels and Acts. After the death and resurrection of Jesus, there was a triangular interaction between Rome, Israel, and the fledgling church. The church became a spiritual hot potato between Rome and the Jews; both tried to control this new movement. The Romans destroyed Israel in AD 70, but the church continued multiplying throughout the empire. The control-focused Romans intensified the persecution. As we see today, though the church is a spiritual kingdom, many earthly kingdoms yearn to rule it.

See how significant location is in the NT:

- Joseph and Mary fled to Egypt so King Herod's forces would not kill their child.
- During his ministry, Jesus frequently moved in and out of Jerusalem. When he was in the city, the authorities tried to kill him. Eventually, they succeeded.
- Jesus roamed in a very confined area. He lived in the rural northern region of Galilee for most of his life. He may have walked over 3,000 miles during the three years of his earthly ministry and perhaps 21,000 miles total. But the extent of his travels was only 300 miles, including his family's escape to Egypt. Otherwise, the maximum north-south distance he traveled was around 120 miles. Americans will drive that distance to go to a mall or a ball game.
- Jesus performed his miracles in specific places, often central to the miracles themselves. He calmed storms on a lake (the Sea of Galilee) known for sudden, violent storms. See Matthew 8:23-34; 9:1ff.
- Jesus celebrated the Lord's Supper in a specific room (nicknamed the Upper Room). John 13:1-5, 12, 21-31.

- On his final trip to Jerusalem, Jesus was arrested, tortured, incarcerated, and executed by crucifixion. Where was he killed? At a specific place called Golgotha. It was located outside the city walls, as prophesied. God tied our salvation to a particular act at an exact location: Golgotha.
- Jesus was buried in a specific tomb, not a mass grave.
- Jesus ascended to heaven from a specific place, the Mount of Olives in eastern Jerusalem.
- Acts 1:8 gives us the structure of the book of Acts; as the book progresses, the Gospel will spread from Jerusalem to Samaria to the regions of the Roman Empire. It's no accident that the book ends when Paul arrives in Rome, the empire's capital. From there, the Gospel will spread to the world.
- In Acts 2, on the Day of Pentecost in the Jewish calendar, people from around the Roman Empire assembled in Jerusalem, and the Holy Spirit descended upon the church.
- Acts 28: Acts ends with the Gospel arriving in Rome, the capital of the Empire. From there, it continued to permeate the empire and even spread to China. God fulfilled the prophecy of Acts 1:8.
- The Epistles (Romans, Ephesians, 1 Peter, etc.) were letters by the apostles to people in specific communities. The issues in the books related to the spiritual and practical conditions in the churches and their communities. For example, Corinth had extensive prostitution and other immoralities, and Corinthian believers sometimes participated. Paul rebuked them.
- Revelation is full of highly significant locations associated with the past, present, and future. It speaks of the nations and geographies of the End Times. A supernatural army will come from the East. John speaks

of the *four corners of the earth* (7:1; 20:8). The kings of the
earth are assembled at Armageddon (16:16). The name
Armageddon means Mount Megiddo, one of the points
overlooking the valley of the battle. Napoleon said that
the armies of the world could assemble there. (Scholars
debate whether the description is symbolic, but it is tied
to an actual location.)

• Revelation describes heaven itself as a place. It has a
throne, a river, trees, walls, and gates. Eternity is
tangible.

YESTERDAY, TODAY, AND TOMORROW

In our modern times, we take tours to the "Holy Land." In the
Bible, that's the place where God chose to have His earthly
dwelling: Israel, specifically the Temple in Jerusalem. But today,
the Holy Spirit resides in all believers, so he has brought the Holy
Land to our hearts.

After the New Testament came to an end, the church grew
around the world. Church history is vividly geographical as time
intersects place. The Gospel has touched every continent. Recent
centuries have seen the rise of "modern missions," such as
England's William Carey going to India. Believers in the Andes are
going to the nations. The Back to Jerusalem movement believes
that God will take the Gospel back through Asia to Jerusalem,
partly using the Silk Road route. Other nationalities are reaching
countries that are hard for Americans to enter. The evangelization
of the world requires believers of *all nations* to work in tandem. It's
not a task given to believers from only one country.

Just as persecution propelled the church through the Roman
Empire, God uses persecution to spread the Gospel today. More
people have been persecuted in the last 100 years than in all the
years of church history before.

When we finish our mission on earth, a tangible destination

awaits--Heaven. When our loved ones die, they finally find their place of permanent peace. It's a location of no death, illness, sickness, war, or violence. But it has beauty and unending joy and jewels and food. (I'm hoping they serve guacamole.)

God made us for a place we can touch and experience. It's the city that we all long for.

LOOKING FOR LOCATION IN ALL THE RIGHT PLACES

Here's a checklist of questions to help you glean insights into the location of your passage and its purpose in the Bible:

1. Where are the characters located?
2. If they are moving, where are they going? Why are they moving there? How are they moving? What direction are they going? How fast are they going?
3. What does the name of the location mean?
4. What spiritual characteristics are the people known for, good or bad? (For example, the Bereans were good!)
5. How does the location relate to God's plan?
6. What has happened of spiritual significance in that place before?
7. What happens along the way of the journey? How does it manifest their spiritual character?
8. What impact will this new place have on their spiritual life? What's its reputation?
9. Is the move part of God's plan or part of their rebellion? (Jonah and the whale!)
10. Will the move take them closer to or further away from God's heart?
11. What can we learn about them by their geographic choices? For example, Lot and his family wanted to live in Sodom. As wicked as the place was, they didn't want to leave. They were comfortable there.

PRACTICE OBSERVING SITE IN THE BIBLE

If you're doing individual Bible study, choose a passage. What words relate to location or movement? Find the place on a map. Use a Bible dictionary, a Bible encyclopedia, or an Internet search to learn more about it and why it is significant to the story.

For group interaction, take a Bible passage and find the location on a map. Show a map of it on a screen or wall. Tell the group to imagine you're pulling the map to the floor underneath their seats. Everyone in the room is sitting somewhere on the map. Now get them thinking about their location. Walk them through the story's movement using the "floor map." Where are the Bible characters, or where are they going on their journey?

PARTING THOUGHTS

Location is geography; it's where people are.

God has always worked in and through geography.

To understand the Bible, you have to understand its basic geography.

Get in the habit of identifying what words in your passage refer to the location and why that location is significant.

The "Holy Land" is where God chose to have His earthly dwelling in Bible times. Where is the Holy Land now?

What would it look like to make a spiritual map of our areas (like a spiritual heat map)?

The intersection of your life and location:

You can't think about Bible locations without wondering how God's plan and geography have related to your own life. Your story is intimately related to geography--even if you've never moved. Some people stay in one place all of their lives. Others move constantly, like the wind. What has God done with your life? Have you seen the reasons yet? Have you wrestled with God over where he's taken you?

Have you ever been upset with God for where he put you, only to realize later that it was the best thing?

Are you moving in some direction? If so, which way? Where is your place?

What geographical choices are you facing now? What spiritual principles seem to apply to your decision?

Are you able to have peace with a location change? Asked another way, *Is there anywhere you can go where God is not there and cannot be trusted?*

Abraham had a massive faith test to uproot from his home city and move to a place God "would" show him. God didn't tell him in advance where he was going. The unseen is unnerving. But Abraham obeyed, and God led him to that strategic land we call Israel (or Palestine). As long as he lived, though, it would never be his permanent home. He awaited heaven for that.

And, as Abraham found, our current place might be okay, but we ache for heaven! Faith tells us we'll get there someday when God is ready.

Until then, can we be at peace where God places us?

Chapter 12
Setting: Context

S etting is the biblical, historical, cultural, and immediate context.

"… it shall greatly help you to understand Scripture, if you mark not only what is spoken or written, but of whom, and unto whom, with what words, at what time, where, to what intent, with what circumstance, considering what goes before, and what follows after."

—Miles Coverdale, in the preface to his English Bible translation, 1535 (English updated)

WHAT IS CONTEXT?

Imagine a preacher telling the congregation, *Hear what the Scripture says: 'Judas … went and hanged himself;' Scripture also says, 'Go and do likewise.'* The preacher is quoting Matthew 27:5 and Luke 10:37 word for word, right? But he has mangled the context.

This chapter explores the critical realm of context, also known as setting. Setting means the surroundings and circumstances of something. In other words, its environment. In Bible study, it's more commonly spoken of as "context." Everything—including every Bible verse—has a context.

In its origin, the word "context" has the idea of weaving together or constructing a text. The parts "fit." The arrangement makes logical sense. Context is not tricky. Nor is it something you must learn now. You've been learning it since you began to speak and interact with others. It comes naturally.

Context determines the meaning of something. For example, consider the English word run. Note how different each of these statements is:

- *Go for a run.*
- *Gotta run.*
- *Got a run.*
- *Got the runs.*

We determine the meaning of each use of "run" by the context.

Bible students toss around the word context frequently, but someone who wrestles with the Bible as a wall of words may be fuzzy about what people mean by the term. No verse in the Bible exists on an island by itself. Other Scriptures surround it and help explain its meaning. Looking at the surrounding context may help you grasp even the hard-to-understand verses. We can't understand a passage correctly without studying the Bible in context. Otherwise, we might misapply it in our lives and teach something wrong to others.

Why is context important? Consider a classic example from Leviticus. When I taught high school students, I was frequently asked, *Mr. Webb, does the Bible talk about tattoos? Is it sinful to get one?* I would take the student to the "tattoo" passage, Leviticus 19:27. In this verse, Moses addresses tattoos and the practice of cutting oneself for the dead. These were practices of the Canaanites, who lived where Moses was about to lead the Israelites.

The tattoo question is apt for introducing this topic because context—like tattoos—has been a thorny subject for Christians. The answer to the tattoo question is very much dependent upon Scriptural context and interpretation. (My perspective is that the tattoo prohibition was a limitation in the Law of Moses to distinguish the Israelites from the pagans around them. It is a gray area Romans 14 issue today; in other words, how is God leading your conscience on the question?)

Our hot-topic debates almost always come down to context. Tattoos, the role of women in the church, hair coverings, drinking, dancing, homosexuality, self-defense, gender, speaking in tongues, snake handling, church structure, End Times, sovereign election, the nature of the United States, etc., etc., all relate to context and biblical interpretation. When applying these verses, we must understand and handle the context faithfully. Further study of the context will help explain many apparent contradictions in the Bible.

We must look at all of God's word to accurately understand its teachings and apply them to our lives. 2 Timothy 2:15 is clear: *Do your best to present yourself to God as one approved, a worker who has no need to be ashamed, rightly handling the word of truth.*

In Bible study, context is looking at a Scriptural verse or passage and comparing it with its section and surroundings. We teach people pieces of the Bible, but they also need the big picture, like the picture on the top of a puzzle box. It shows how all of the pieces fit together. You can't pull one out and try to make it match another hole. Even the individual books in the Bible aren't on islands by themselves. They have their meaning in association with one another. We can't simply plop down, open to a random verse, pluck it out of the surrounding context, and be confident we understand it fully and are using it correctly.

Each verse is in the context of a paragraph or section. Each section is in the context of a chapter or book. Each chapter is in the context of its book and similar books (such as the other Gospels). Each book is in the context of its Testament (Old or New) and of the entire Bible. Each verse or concept is also in the context of parallel or similar statements in the Bible.

It might help you to look at it as "circles of context" that wrap around the verse:

1. The same topic or term in the same immediate context (such as its paragraph).

2. The same topic or term in the same biblical book.

3. The same topic or term by the same author.

4. The same topic or term in the period, genre, or Testament.

5. The same topic or term in the Bible as a whole.

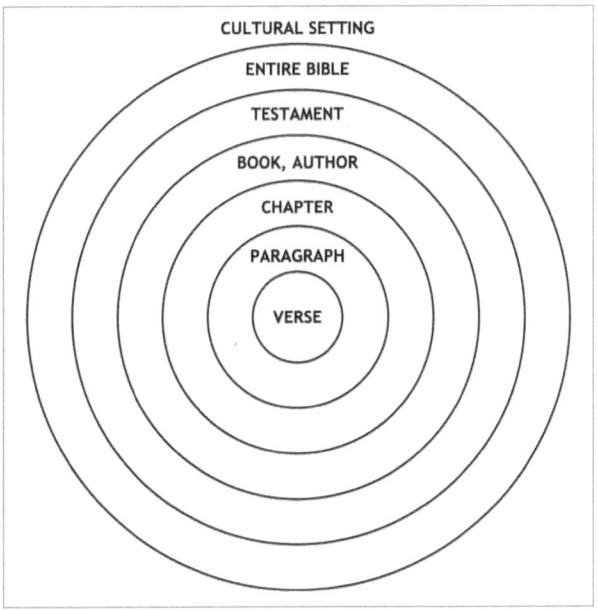

You can answer many of your questions about a passage by reading the text around it. Reading the text involves looking at the near context (the verses immediately before and after) and the far context (the paragraph or the chapter preceding or following the passage you're studying). The book, the Testament (Old or New) and the Bible itself are part of the context. And each writer has his own "environment." There will be things important to him, and there may be words and concepts that he favors. For example, Paul uses the Greek word *pas* (typically translated as "all" or "every") 464 times in his epistles.

We can't talk about context without mentioning other "C" words. Correlation is comparing Scriptures with other Scriptures to see how they clarify each other and add to your understanding. The Scriptures together will flesh out each other. You can use a concordance to see the different uses of a word in the Bible; a concordance is an alphabetical listing of words in the Bible and the passages where you'll find them. You can buy a concordance, but if you have a Bible software program, it will have a built-in concordance feature. Online, search for Bible concordance and you'll find plenty of free options.

Another "C" word is culture. The Bible was lived and compiled thousands of years ago in cultural environments that were different than ours. Understanding the cultural background of your passage may shed light on things that confuse you. For example, various practices were used in ancient times for ratifying a covenant. An animal could be sliced in two (with a veiled threat against breaking the agreement). Another way was to place one's hand under the other party's thigh. You'll agree that signing with a pen is less complicated than either of these!

I recommend that you check out the *Cultural Backgrounds Study Bible*. It's an insightful resource and comes in different translations.

WHAT DOES IT MEAN TO BE "IN CONTEXT"?

Context has both a positive side and a negative side. On the positive, you can better understand a verse by looking at the surrounding context. On the negative, you can better avoid misapplications.

If something is "in context" or put "into context," it fits with all of the surroundings words, verses, circumstances, and logical points. It is not floating around by itself; it has some role to play in the author's argument.

Don't forget that context is about understanding what the writer meant, not what the passage "means to you." What it means to you is the application, which we'll get to in the chapter on spark.

WHAT DOES IT MEAN TO BE "OUT OF CONTEXT"?

When we say a verse is taken "out of context," we mean it is used for a purpose that doesn't fit with the writer's argument. In effect, it contradicts the purpose of the writing. It means something different from the writer's intended meaning. What is the problem with looking at verses out of context? Because they don't say what you're using them to say, you are damaging the word of God and misleading yourself and others. You're also fueling the flame of unedifying dispute.

Quotes can easily be manipulated and used out of context. Movie promotions do this all of the time. They will pull a quote out of a review and say something like, *You won't want to leave!* when the full statement is, *You won't want to leave the lobby and have to watch the movie!* The same thing happens on the Internet: Memes are notorious for showing data out of context. We like to stick to our favorite opinions and often take things out of context. Let's not do that with Scripture. God cautions us to handle it rightly.

HELPFUL QUESTIONS TO ASK TO UNDERSTAND THE CONTEXT

Here are some questions that will help you better understand the context of the passage in front of you:

PERSONAL

- Who is the writer or the speaker?
- What do we know about this person (story, reputation, values, passions, etc.)?
- Who is the audience, and what were the circumstances?

LITERARY

- What was said immediately before and after the verse?
- What did the author say elsewhere on the same subject?
- What do other biblical authors say on the same subject?
- How did the original hearers understand the message and respond to it?
- What is the rest of the paragraph or book?
- Who or what is the subject in the current context?
- If the writer uses a word such as "that" or "this," what is he referring to?

HISTORICAL

- In what period in history were these people living?
- What was happening in their region?

- What was the dominant empire(s)?

CULTURAL

- What was going on politically, economically, culturally, and religiously at the time?
- What type of society was it? (Understand the culture, and you understand the meaning of the words and statements more fully. Was it a tribal culture? One that valued the honor of the tribe over the righteousness of an individual?)

GEOGRAPHICAL

- Where does it take place?
- How does the geography (terrain, location) add significance to the story? (For example, even when further north than Jerusalem, they went "up" to Jerusalem. It was because of the higher elevation of Jerusalem, a city on a hill.)

THEOLOGICAL

- What is the author trying to say about all this?
- What did the author know about God? What did the audience know about God? How did they worship Him? Were they worshiping something else?

- Where and how does this piece of Scripture fit into the progression of the Scriptures?

AVOID PROOF-TEXTING

Proof-texting is when we use isolated, out-of-context verses or passages supposedly to prove an argument or point of doctrine. The context of a verse, who wrote it, the period in which it was written, where they wrote it, etc., all need to be understood if we are going to know what God intended it to convey. Make sure that the context bears out your use of the verse. Don't make false conclusions with the word of God. Keep your interpretations in alignment with the point of the passage.

THE BIBLE AND ITS DIFFERENT CONTEXTS

The authors wrote each book of the Bible at a specific time in history. Recognize who wrote the book and what was happening in his world then.

- Who was in power?
- What was the spiritual condition of God's people at the time? Who were their leaders?
- In the passage, were the people turning toward or away from God?
- What purpose does this paragraph have in the author's argument?

What form of literature is your passage? Bible passages can be:

- Historical/narrative (story). A staggering seventy-five percent of the Bible is story.
- Poetic. Thirty percent of the Old Testament is poetry.

- Prophetic. Twenty percent of the Bible was prophetic at the time of writing.
- Gospel.
- Teaching (also known as didactic). Romans is the prime example.

OLD TESTAMENT

Testament means "covenant." Most of the Old Testament (Covenant) refers to the experience of Israel under the Law of Moses. The exception is the period from creation to the Red Sea crossing. A command given in the context of the Law of Moses does not apply to you today. (If it's a moral issue, though, the principle still applies because it flows from the holiness of God.)

HISTORY

The first seventeen books of the OT are books of history, full of stories about God's relationship with humanity and the relationship of humans with other humans. Those stories have distinct cultural backgrounds, which explains why some things might seem bizarre to us but were common back then.

For example, Genesis 15:9-21 describes an event that seems very strange to us. Several animals were cut in half, and a flaming torch moved through the pieces. In that culture, a contract was sealed by cutting up animals and having the participants walk through the parts. (It conveyed a subtle threat to the person who might wish to break the contract.) So God was using a common legal practice. And the fact that Abram was asleep showed that God's promise was unilateral. In other words, it was one-sided. God was binding Himself to the covenant.

. . .

POETRY

Structure is vital in poetry. In Biblical Hebrew, poems rhymed with thoughts rather than sounds. You may see two lines that seem to say the same thing but with different words. That's called synonymous parallelism. If they express an opposite thought, it's called antithetical parallelism. Sometimes the next thought builds on the first (synthetic parallelism). The context may be emphasizing the point.

The book of Proverbs revolves around specific themes, such as friendship and diligence. They are general statements of wisdom, mainly from King Solomon. As you look at the book, pretend you are a detective looking for the occurrences of a particular theme. How would you creatively stage Proverbs?

Ecclesiastes, also by King Solomon, has a spiral structure, spiraling around various themes related to the vanity of mortal life. The book should drive you toward deeper contemplation of the meaning of your life. What truly matters in our human existence?

PROPHETS

There are seventeen prophetic books in the OT. The five "Major Prophets" are called such because they are larger. The Minor Prophets are shorter. Each book has a historical context. For example, Nahum is a prophecy against the kingdom of Assyria, pronouncing its condemnation. In general, each book gives messages of judgment and restoration. For more on the prophets, see the chapter on Bible book summaries.

NEW TESTAMENT

GOSPELS AND ACTS

The "Gospels" are the first four books of the New Testament. They tell the story of Jesus, with each of the four writers (Matthew, Mark, Luke, and John) putting his cultural background and emphasis on the account.

Jesus said some ambiguous and difficult things, many of which we may not fully understand until we see him. He also said simple and clear things; I recommend starting with these.

Jesus began to give parables when the rejection of him intensified. He intended the parable's message to be understood by people of faith, with the hostile people being blind to it. And each parable expresses a central point; we shouldn't make too much out of the details because they supplement the story. We wouldn't want to build a primary doctrine on a parable.

Luke wrote the Gospel of Luke to an individual, a Roman official named Theophilus. Luke also wrote the book of Acts to Theophilus, so the Gospel can be considered "Luke Volume I" and Acts "Luke Volume II."

EPISTLES

Epistle means "letter." The books from Romans to Revelation were letters written by an apostle (Paul, John, Peter, etc.) to a person or group.

Romans is an intense book. To understand it, you must start from the beginning and progressively follow Paul's chain of logic. Whatever verse you are in is tightly connected to its context before and after, so its meaning will come from that context.

Sometimes it appears there are contradictions. For example, in Ephesians 2:4-10, Paul says, *By grace you have saved through faith . . . not as a result of works.* But he also says, *Work out your own salvation with fear and trembling* (Philippians 2:12). The latter verse does not mean that works save you but that they express your salvation. It's similar to what James meant when he said faith without works is dead (James 2:17). True faith produces fruit. Context helps resolve apparent contradictions.

REVELATION

Revelation has been giving people fits for the last 2,000 years, so don't feel bad if it blows your mind, also! As you read the book, keep the concept of context close to mind.

The Apostle John wrote the book during an era of intense persecution in the Roman Empire. He urged the believers to endure faithfully. He gave them the hope that God would not forget their service and that they were heading toward an eternal reward.

John contrasts two kingdoms that have long been in opposition. The first is the Kingdom of God, which will emerge victorious. The Lamb, also known as the King of Kings and Lord of Lords, will rule all creation for eternity.

The other kingdom is that of Satan. John describes it as Babylon, the place of rebellion. Satan and his kingdom are on an express train bound for the Lake of Fire.

For the faithful servants of God, things would get messy and painful for a while, but God would win. And we'll join the eternal party when our time on earth is over.

Revelation 2-3 is the famous "Letters to Seven Churches" section, in which the Apostle John wrote to seven churches addressing specific circumstances. They were actual churches in real locations. In Rev. 3:15–16, the church in Laodicea is said to be *neither cold nor hot*. This spiritual point comes from their geographic context. Two nearby towns had hot and cold springs, but the water in Laodicea was lukewarm, without taste, and useless. And that's how John describes their church. With some creativity, you could develop a fascinating stage play on the seven churches.

SOME EXAMPLES TO CHEW ON

Ponder the verses below and see if you can explain them without input from other verses. Then, study their contexts to see how setting helps with biblical understanding.

- Luke 9:1, compared with Luke 22:36.
- 2 Chronicles 7:14.

PARTING THOUGHTS

Context is one of your most powerful tools for understanding. You can't correctly interpret without understanding the context.

Every Bible verse has a context! In what part of the Bible is your passage? Knowing its context will help you tremendously.

Compare Scriptures to see how they relate and help you understand the whole Bible.

Remember: Context is king! There's a logical flow to the books of the Bible, and context will help you sort it out.

Chapter 13
Sequence: Timing, Logic

S*equence refers to the words of timing and logical flow.*

There will never be a story more moving to the believer than that of the final few days of Jesus on earth. You know what's going to happen step-by-step, yet each time you watch it, the agony is freshly wrenching.

You want to kidnap Judas on his way out of the Upper Room. You yearn to wrap your arms around Jesus in the Garden of Gethsemane. If you could, you'd grab Pilate by the shoulders, slap him silly, and make him live up to what he knows is right. Yet, each time you hear the story, the train rolls towards its barbarous wreck.

The story of the last week of Jesus's life is, in short, a foul feast of sequences. The treatment of Christ gets increasingly barbaric while his love for humanity intensifies. The dialogue drifts from spiritually deep to savagely cynical to supernaturally poignant. By the end, Jesus is forgiving all of us and giving up his spirit.

Want to hear one of the most potent tips for Bible understanding? Pay close attention to the sequencing of the verses.

Sequence refers to events (or actions, ideas, numbers, etc.) that have a specific order and lead to a particular result. It means that something leads to something else, and, viewed from the other side, something follows something that came before. A leads to B, and B follows A.

You will see sequence throughout the Bible. Every time I've explored this theme with a group, we've found words of sequence in our verses. Grasp this concept and you'll be able to break down a passage and understand its flow and movement.

We don't pay enough attention to it in Bible study. In the passage before you, what happens when? What happens next? What leads to what? What is the order of the dramatic "beats" of the story? What logical point leads to what logical point?

NEXT IN THE SEQUENCE

Many passages are narrative stories, but some passages are "didactic," which means they teach something. For example, the didactic books (Romans, Galatians, etc.) are primarily letters written by the apostles to local churches or individuals. Each recipient is a group or person with real issues. Sometimes they face external pressures, and sometimes they make bad choices. The issues they face explain the content and logical flow of the letter. That's why Paul fusses at the Corinthians. They were a rowdy bunch from a notorious city, and Paul had to correct their unrighteous practices. So his points and arguments relate to what the Corinthians are facing or doing.

Whether you have a narrative story (such as Moses and the Israelites on the Wilderness Journey) or a teaching book (such as

Romans), you have real people with real situations and a story that progresses step-by-step to make its points.

To give your Bible study a jolt, take your passage and look for the sequence/timing words. Look especially for these types of sequence:

1. Timing.
2. Logic.

Timing refers to the relationship between time and action. It also refers to words that deal with time, such as day, week, year, etc. Here are examples:

But when the fullness of time had come, God sent forth his Son.
—Galatians 4:4

When Jesus had finished all these sayings, he said to his disciples, 'You know that after two days the Passover is coming, and the Son of Man will be delivered up to be crucified.'
—Matthew 26:1-2

Once you start to look for it, you'll be amazed at how much timing appears in the Bible.

Logic is a progression of points or facts from one to another. Each item is based on what came before. If an argument is "logical," that means it is correct and reasonable. Some Bible authors make multiple points in sequence. Perhaps the classic example is Romans 8:28-30: *And we know that for those who love God all things work together for good, for those who are called according to his purpose. For those whom he foreknew he also predestined to be conformed to the image of his Son, in order that he might be the first-born among many brothers. And those whom he predestined he also* *called, and those whom he called he also justified, and those whom he justified he also glorified.*

In the Bible, sometimes timing and logic are put together. But whether they are together or alone, you see "sequence" in almost every verse.

TIME SEQUENCE

Something leads to something. That's sequence. Timing is the relation of the sequence in terms of time.

Think of timing with God's people in the Old and New Testaments. Imagine the sweat on the Israelite brows as they watched the Egyptian army bearing down on them by the Red Sea. God came in at the last minute. Think of the timing of events with Jesus and the disciples. Consider how timing fits with the writers of the Epistles, such as Paul. And think how timing plays such a massive part in Revelation.

God is a God of timing. Whatever he does, he has planned it ahead of time, and he strikes at the exact moment. Theologians speak of Eternity Past and Eternity Future. Being eternal, God has no beginning and no end. What we think of eternity before creation is Eternity Past, and Eternity Future is what happens after God recreates the universe (removing sin and preparing for "forever"). Time as we know it, will be over. But even though he is not time-bound, God invades it like a banshee.

God's timing is precise; he acts when he chooses to, which is typically later than we want. I love Gandalf's words in *The Lord of the Rings: Fellowship of the Ring*; Frodo tells Gandalf he is late, to which Gandalf responds: *A wizard is never late, Frodo Baggins. Nor is he early. He arrives precisely when he means to.* That is God's style.

More than once have I been shocked at the precision of His timing. God is the God of the "close call" (always, not occasionally!). You can't oversell this point about God and timing. God seems to enjoy waiting until the last minute, like the cavalry in a

Western. This seeming delay gives Him greater glory but also drives us finite humans stark raving mad. But he is the sovereign God of the universe, and what he does is the right thing. Always.

Randomly choose a verse in the Bible, and you'll almost always land on one that has sequence in it, in some form. What time sequence words are in the passage you are reading?

SEEING SEQUENCE IN BIBLE PASSAGES: TIMING

Let's note the timing in a short passage in John 13:

> 26 *Jesus answered, 'It is he to whom I will give this morsel of bread when I have dipped it.'*
>
> *So when he had dipped the morsel, he gave it to Judas, the son of Simon Iscariot.*
>
> 27 *Then after he had taken the morsel, Satan entered into him.*
>
> This event happened after Judas took the morsel of bread. "Then" and "after" are time words.
>
> *Jesus said to him, 'What you are going to do, do quickly.'. . .*
>
> "Are going to do" is future. It will happen.
>
> "Quickly" is a word of speed and time. Judas, don't take long.
>
> 30 *So, after receiving the morsel of bread, he immediately went out. And it was night.*

Judas received the bread and *immediately* left. *Night* is a time word. It tells us the time of day and sets up the narrative; Jesus will be arrested and tried at night. In their system, a night trial was illegal. The "Passion of Christ" sequence begins.

Now let's go to a time sequence example in the "Epistles" (letters) of the New Testament. Here again is this short-but-important passage in Galatians (4:4-5):

But when the fullness of time had come, God sent forth his Son, born of woman, born under the law, to redeem those who were under the law, so that we might receive adoption as sons.

When is a word of time. It will lead to something.

Fullness of time means that the time had fully come to make something happen.

Had come means that the point in time had arrived.

Sent forth is past tense; it happened in the past. It has happened; it is a fact.

The purpose of God sending His Son is redemption. It's a logical sequence. Because he sent His Son, we can receive "adoption" and become His children.

Consider the sequencing in Matthew 8:23-27 (the story of Jesus calming the storm on the Sea of Galilee). It's so easy to miss these shifts (beats).

23 And when he got into the boat, his disciples followed him. 24 And behold, there arose a great storm on the sea, so that the boat was being swamped by the waves; but he was asleep.

Time is embedded in this story. Jesus got into the boat first and then came His disciples. They ventured into the midst of the lake (the Sea of Galilee is a vast inland lake, often called a sea because of that), and then the storm came up.

The boat *being swamped* expresses the process; it didn't just get "swamped" at once; it took on water and began to sink. The sinking took a bit of time.

25 And they went and woke him, saying, 'Save us, Lord; we are perishing.'

Seeing the swamping, they became frightened and went to wake up Jesus. One thing led to another. These men were experienced fishermen and used to the sudden and intense storms of the Sea of Galilee. The sea is surrounded on three sides by steep slopes, and wind can come down quickly from the slopes and blow hard across the water. By their reaction, this storm is more powerful than the norm.

Are perishing is also a time statement, if you think about it. It is like saying, *We are in the process of dying from the swamping of the boat; we will drown. It is happening now, and it will lead to our death.*

26 *And he said to them, 'Why are you afraid, O you of little faith?' Then he rose and rebuked the winds and the sea, and there was a great calm.*

He identifies their condition. Their present condition (time) was that of being afraid and not having faith. *Then:* After saying that, he rose. Rising, he rebuked the winds and the sea. Then came a great calm. Calm seas (and winds, of course) resulted from his effort.

27 *And the men marveled, saying, What sort of man is this, that even winds and sea obey him?*

We infer time here. After seeing what Jesus did, the disciples marveled. That was their response to what he did.

They used the present tense: *Winds and sea obey him*. They said it to say that that is the way it always is. Winds and sea are always subject to Jesus.

We see sequence of both time and logic here.

SEEING SEQUENCE IN BIBLE PASSAGES: LOGIC

What about the sequence of logic in the Bible? Let's use Romans 8:18-25 to practice. Look at each sentence. Mark whether the sentence has timing, logic, or both. Circle the appropriate words in the sentence.

> 18 *For I consider that the sufferings of this present time are not worth comparing with the glory that is to be revealed to us.*
>
> 19 *For the creation waits with eager longing for the revealing of the sons of God.* 20 *For the creation was subjected to futility, not willingly, but because of him who subjected it, in hope* 21 *that the creation itself will be set free from its bondage to corruption and obtain the freedom of the glory of the children of God.*
>
> 22 *For we know that the whole creation has been groaning together in the pains of childbirth until now.*
>
> 23 *And not only the creation, but we ourselves, who have the firstfruits of the Spirit, groan inwardly as we wait eagerly for adoption as sons, the redemption of our bodies.*
>
> 24 *For in this hope we were saved. Now hope that is seen is not hope. For who hopes for what he sees?*
>
> 25 *But if we hope for what we do not see, we wait for it with patience.*

Timing and logic often go together, especially in narrative literature (as in the Calming the Storm passage). They certainly go together in the "teaching" books and letters. For example, we know that *we love because he first loved us* (1 John 4:19). Is this referring to time or logic? The answer is, "Yes!" Both!

TEST TIMING ON A RANDOM PASSAGE

You can do this by yourself or make it a group exercise: Say to the group, *Give me a number. Now give me another number. Now give me the name of a Bible book.* Put them all together, and you have a random passage. If you're in a group, have one person read it out loud, with the participants yelling when they hear a word of timing.

PARTING THOUGHTS

I encourage you always to observe what God is doing in a passage through timing. Watch for the shifts. Some are little ones.

Sequence means that one thing leads directly to another. It is related to timing and can refer to timing/time words or logical sequence.

Most verses have timing words! Which words are in the passage you're reading?

God is the Master of precise timing; he acts when he chooses to. Whenever God works, he has planned it ahead of time, and it is the right thing. You could call him the God of the "close call" because he acts when things seem darkest to us.

Every Christian can see God's timing in his or her life. *What's your story? Have you seen Him work through the "close call"?*

Humans are in awe of God for His precise timing when he "comes through," but we are incredibly antsy and faithless when he seems silent. *Can you praise him for his silence? Has he lost his ability to time when things are silent?*

The winter is a time of dormancy, but that doesn't mean nature is entirely at rest. That's when plants are driving roots deeper for growth to come. *Can you thank God for your winters?*

With the will of God in our lives, we tend to focus on the "what." (At any given time, most Christians that I know are fretting over "the next step in their lives.") But "timing" is just as significant as the "what." One miracle of God is how he coordinates all of our timing together.

We should look more for God's timing.

If the timing is right, his "what" will come.

Chapter 14
Speaking: Sound, Emphasis

S peaking means the insight that comes from sounding out the passage and even changing emphasis.

But be doers of the word, and not hearers only, deceiving yourselves.
—James 1:22

How important is sound? Imagine the result if you blended the soundtrack from *Jaws* into a Hallmark movie! The type of music used for a scene makes all the difference in your emotional response.

It's fantastic that we have the Bible in black-and-white print for the world to read. But the words passively sitting there must be brought to life by our minds and voices. What we do with them is a choice.

When the Bible is a "wall" to people, they see black-and-white words on a page but have trouble cracking the surface. One fabulous way to change that is to convert the words to sounds. Read the verse out loud. Doing so works well because many people learn better by listening than by reading.

Can you think of a Bible passage in which sound makes a big difference? (Hint: 1 Kings 19; Revelation 4-6.) The way we emphasize words sends a message. When we read or speak something out loud, meaning is conveyed not only by the words but through sound and emphasis. What if we change the sound? What if we modulate our voice, adjust the volume, change the tone, or emphasize a different word or syllable? Will intonation affect how we perceive the meaning?

Usually, we speak with inflection and naturally emphasize words or syllables. We do it without even thinking about it. I've heard that ninety percent of what we convey in our speech comes from our tone of voice. People call you a robot if you read aloud in total monotone.

Here's a revealing experiment: Read John 3:16 out loud in total monotone, robot-like. Then read it as you usually do. Do it three times. What syllables or words did you emphasize? You probably tend to emphasize the same ones each time but don't realize that until someone points it out to you.

Now reread the verse, but emphasize a different syllable. Then read it several more times, each time highlighting a different syllable or word.

If you change what you emphasize, you'll see it differently. By definition, you can't highlight everything. You have to pick and choose. In making a choice, you convey meaning to the sentence or verse. You'd perceive it differently if you changed your choice by emphasizing a different word.

If the Bible is a wall of words to you, try sounding out some verses and changing the emphasized word each time you do. You'll get out of your rut and gain new insight. Why not practice that right now? And why not make it fun: Take your Bible and open it to a random page. Close your eyes and randomly place your finger on the page. Read the verse out loud as you usually might. Now, intentionally change the words/syllables you emphasize. What do you see in the verse as you change the pattern?

Our goal in this process is not to change the meaning God intended but to better understand what that meaning is. And to help ourselves get engaged in his word.

HOW TO IMPROVE YOUR VERBAL SKILLS

In my college days at Florida State, I took a class titled "Oral Interpretation of Prose." Our textbook had random selections of literature, ancient and modern. Each night, we'd get in front of our group and practice reading a paragraph out loud. The instructors pushed us to put more and more emotion, expression, intonation, and variety into what we read. By the end of the course, I felt like I was an actor on a Broadway stage.

The process felt weird initially, but that class left a mark on me that continues today. Never again would I dare to read a Bible passage out loud without bringing expression to the reading. That commitment has impacted thousands of people.

The experience was also a crucial part of my developing this program. It laid a foundation for looking at the Bible creatively and expressively. Gradually I built the blocks that would become *Awake from Bible Slumber*.

In previous chapters, we discussed the principles of story and drama. When you watch a movie or a play, you know when someone is acting naturally and "nailing it." Her character feels authentic. It seems real. But lousy acting is stilted. The actor emphasizes the wrong things. The intonation is stiff. You know it when you hear it.

When dramatizing a story, you must think of what to emphasize verbally. You must intentionally use syllable emphasis, pauses, pitch, and even quietness.

So when you read a passage out loud (at home, at church, or wherever), use emphasis. Here are some things you can vary:

- Speed of your speech.
- Tone of voice.
- Pitch, high and low/deep.
- Modulation. Raising and lowering your voice.
- Volume, loud or soft. (Which makes more impact: Loud or soft?)
- Pauses. Pausing is the hidden gem of speech technique.
- Inflection. Emphasize different syllables and notice the change.
- Non-verbal communication/body language.

THE BIBLE AND SOUND

If we read the Bible with the same passion with which we'd read the newspaper, we drain the flavor out of the Scriptures. But the Bible is the word of God! It's living and active. It is sharper than a double-edged sword and slices our souls with surgical precision.

So reject monotone! Let the passage soak in your mind, pray for enlightenment from the Holy Spirit, notice the passion behind the words, and speak them as if you mean them. Bring the same passion to the reading that you see in the writing. Bring the stories to life!

When I prepare to read a section of Scripture at church, I pray, soak in the passage for a while, and then observe. And I'll read it out loud in different ways and notice how it sounds. Things pop to the surface, especially what appears to be emphasized. I also pick up on the comparisons and contrasts in the passage.

GO AUDIO WITH YOUR BIBLE

We are blessed to have audio resources that portray the verbal richness of reading the Bible with more dramatic emphasis. Some audio Bibles have bland readers. Try listening to a different Bible version and other readers. Two of my favorites are the Bible readings of Max McLean (www.bibleonstage.org) and *The Bible Experience*. You can't beat Denzel and Paulette Washington's version of Song of Solomon (in *The Bible Experience*) or Max McLean on Psalm 22. McLean has a voice of divine butterscotch.

ORALITY: GETTING THE BIBLE TO THOSE WHO CANNOT—OR PREFER NOT TO—READ

We can't discuss God's spoken word without touching on "orality." Orality is when a society expresses itself verbally because writing and print are generally unavailable.

It's time to wake up to the significance of orality. Some two-thirds of the world learn orally. Even in societies where people can read, they may prefer to hear things instead of read them. Most Westerners prefer to watch a movie than read a book.

Here's how sound-focused Americans are:

- Up to four-fifths of U.S. learners are oral.
- Over half of Americans will never read another book after high school.
- A majority of people over the age of 16 are functionally illiterate.
- More than three-fourths of U.S. households do not buy or read books.
- A literacy survey in the U.S. in 1992 found that 90 million adults have difficulty using the written word to accomplish everyday tasks consistently and accurately. Yet almost all of them can read.

The implications for discipleship are staggering. The first thing we give a new disciple is a book. Is that the best approach? What if we've been doing it wrong?

International missions experts are exploring the concept of orality and how it applies to spreading the Gospel because many people in developing nations do not read well. They don't necessarily want to learn to read and write, and training them takes a long time. What if attempts to teach literacy instead cause the initial Gospel outreach to stumble?

People love to hear stories and, in many cultures, will memorize them word for word. I've mentioned that three-fourths of the Bible itself is story-based. Ancient cultures focused on stories, and so do many contemporary societies. If God wired people to hear the Gospel with stories, we should use them more in our evangelism. Some mission organizations do just that, telling Bible stories with their service projects. There are some one hundred stories used for this purpose. The hearers take the stories (and principles) back to their villages. The stories engage the people in the theology of the Bible without mentioning the word theology itself. Discipleship begins to grow.

The Bible stories fit very well into cultures that prioritize hospitality, honor/shame dynamics, and the value of the community ("tribe") over the individual. They pick up on subtleties in the biblical story that we Westerners cannot fully process. They also share stories in a group context so the message rapidly spreads (whereas a reading-focused society communicates one-to-one). Not only will more people hear the word, but by hearing it orally, they will retain more of it. Oral learners have a superior potential for memorizing the Bible.

Most of the people in Bible times were oral. The Scriptures were verbally transmitted before they were written and distributed. The disciples heard and memorized Jesus's words. Paul dictated his letters, which were read aloud to the churches. It's thought that only one-tenth of New Testament believers were literate. The original hearers of the Scriptures would have understood the stories as dramas. Research on the Gospel of Mark indicates that it contains reader notations, telling the reader how to read a passage to the assembly. Hebrews 1:2 says that in these last days, God has *spoken* to us by his Son. Fascinating, isn't it?

Until recent centuries, most people in the church could not read. The church had to emphasize oral reading in the service for hundreds of years. Priests and ministers would read and expound the Scriptures to the congregants. Liturgy-focused churches read from at least four sections of the Bible in each service, and they also recite the historic creeds responsively. Such services enable non-readers to absorb the word.

As the world has shifted toward digital communication, in many ways it has moved from linear, analytical/logical thinking toward non-linear, random thinking. Learning is based more on interaction than reading or lectures. And rather than merely searching for knowledge, the thinker also searches for significance. The *Awake from Bible Slumber* approach is perfect for this person.

An emerging and exciting field of study is Biblical Performance Criticism (BPC). BPC leverages the power of orality and the oral background of the Bible; in BPC, Bible students absorb a biblical text and then perform it. (Welcome to making the Bible come alive!) I expect to see great fruit from BPC in the years ahead.

LET'S PRACTICE OUR SPEAKING!

Here are some suggestions for practicing your verbal reading of the Bible.

- Do a sample reading of a dramatic passage, with emphasis.

- Use a random system to choose the passage.
- Before reading verbally, read the passage silently; soak it in; creatively observe it.
- Read a verse multiple times and emphasize a different word each time.
- Play a selection of audio Bible.
- Read a passage verbally with several people, going around the circle, one verse after another; practice varying the emphasis of words and learn from each other.

BIBLE EXAMPLES TO TRY

Here are some significant statements and dialogues in the Bible. How would you enunciate them? If you're in a group, have each member give their take.

- *My God, my God, why have you forsaken me?* (Matthew 27:46; spoken by Jesus when dying on the cross.)
- *What is truth?* (John 18:38; spoken by Governor Pontius Pilate when deciding whether to execute Jesus.)
- 1 Kings 19:13; God speaking to Elijah, who ran in panic from Jezebel.
- Jesus on the boat, preaching to the crowd on shore. Or preaching to the crowd on the mount. He had to project.
- Matthew 16:13, 15; Jesus to the disciples, at Caesarea Philippi.
- Acts 9:5-6; the interaction between Jesus and Saul on the Damascus Road.

PARTING THOUGHTS

Meaning is conveyed by what we emphasize. (By definition, you can't emphasize everything!)

As you read a passage, practicing changing the emphasis will help you see it differently, which can help you gain new understanding. You may be surprised and blessed.

The Bible gives several clues about what is emphasized, such as choice of words, repetition, and word order/placement. Look closely at these.

What once was verbal is now in written form in the Bible. We should take it back to verbal more than we do.

Our goal is not to change the meaning God intended but to better understand what that meaning is.

People who work in missions have realized the significance and impact of orality in cultures worldwide. And they've realized that it's important in American culture, too.

As we talk about making the Bible come alive, we must spend more time exploring the concepts, methods, and implications of "speaking." We have overlooked just how sound-focused our culture is. Orality in the U.S. and worldwide may be one of the finest tools for discipleship in the days ahead.

Think how you can use orality to reach your friends.

And practice the power of variety as you read the Bible!

Chapter 15
Spark: Application

S park asks, *What are the principles of the passage, and how can you apply them in your life?*

There is no discovery of the truth of Christ's teaching, no unanswerable inward endorsement of it, without committing oneself to his way of life.
—J. B. Phillips

The goal of your Christian life is to know God and glorify Him daily. That means opening every nook of your life to his holiness and glory and doing what his word says. We can't be like one group I heard about, who had a reputation for talking theology all day long without it making a whit of difference in their lives.

Just as faith without works is *dead* (James 2:17), and mere words are useless, we must take our learning to the next level. It must impact our walk with God. It must motivate us to be Christ-like, to love God more, and to treat others with His grace. We must learn how he thinks and acts and how we should respond.

This final chapter is about applying what we've extracted from the Bible.

James tells us to be doers of the word and not hearers only (James 1:22). After we have observed a passage and interpreted or understood it to the best of our ability, application is putting to use the concepts we have learned. It is living out the messages and principles we see in the Scriptural stories and teachings.

Bible study should produce "outcomes." Outcomes are changes in knowledge, attitude, speech, and behavior. We should become increasingly Christlike and more like the humans God designed us to be--honorable and joined closely with our Creator.

Christ showed us the way. He fed on the word, constantly communed with the Father, and lived the truth every moment. *What response does the word spark in me?*

LEVELS OF APPLICATION

When it comes to Bible study and application, I've found it helpful to imagine three levels:

1. The first level is foundational; it's the level of story/passage. It's the words of Scripture at face value, without injecting interpretation or theology. *Awake from Bible Slumber* is focused on this level: Gaining clarity on what the word is saying. Here, it's critical to think of the original audience for the passage. Does the message apply only to them or to us also?

2. At the second level are the principles/truths of the passage. If the passage contains a special situation that does not directly apply to you (such as parting the water of the Red Sea), what principles can you take away from it? Look for a small number of principles rather than trying to make something out of each word.

3. At the third level, the highest, is the application: How do you use that principle/truth in your daily living and decision-making? Be specific.

Simply charted, here are the three levels, as if floors of a building:

APPLICATION OF THE PASSAGE
PRINCIPLES OF THE PASSAGE
WORDS OF THE PASSAGE

Now, let's explain the three levels:

THE FOUNDATIONAL LEVEL: THE PASSAGE ITSELF

At the foundational level, we absorb the passage and observe it. We are not jumping to theology or points of interpretation. Those will come later.

Use Bible study resources to help you navigate Level 1 and increase your understanding of the passage. The more you can use, the better. Out of the many excellent ones available, here is a sampling:

- Bible dictionaries and lexicons help you learn more about the individual words and names.
- Bible encyclopedias give more in-depth information on the words, places, and topics.
- Study Bibles are Bibles with helpful notes included. You'll be amazed at how much information they contain; some have 80,000 notes. Highly-regarded study Bibles include *The NIV Study Bible*, *The ESV Study Bible*,

The Life Application Study Bible, The MacArthur Study Bible, and *The NET Bible.* I recommend you visit a bookstore to look at these and others in person. Remember that a study Bible may come with different translations. You have to make two decisions: Translation of choice and study version of choice.

- Concordances are books that list the uses of a word in the Bible. For example, a concordance will tell you all the times that "faith" occurs.

- Commentaries help you understand the meaning of a passage through the writer's informed comments. Commentaries vary greatly in quality and helpfulness, so do further research before buying them.

- Bible software, such as Accordance or Logos. Both programs are enormously powerful. They have inexpensive starter packages and charge for add-ons. Accordance is my constant companion; it's available on Mac, iPhone, iPad, Windows, and Android. Check out these software options at www.accordancebible.com and www.logos.com.

- Bible study websites, such as www.bible.org, www. blueletterbible.org, www.biblegateway.com, and www. bible.com. These give you study options short of buying software. The downside is that you must have an Internet connection to use them. The software programs will have more extensive resources and be quicker to use, but they'll be much more expensive.

- A well-stocked Christian bookstore. There's nothing like getting hands-on with the options, and the staff should be able to guide you through the choices. As you search for resources, please visit your local Christian bookstore.

- The Christian Book website, www.christianbook.com. CB has been providing great tools at great prices for decades.

THE SECOND LEVEL: THE PRINCIPLES/TRUTHS

You can't interpret correctly without a solid foundation of observation. The observation process will surface items that you want to understand better. Interpretation is the next step, exploring what the author intended the passage to mean.

To whom was the message originally given? Does it apply directly to you? If it doesn't, go up to the second level and see if there is a universal principle or concept that applies to you. Level 2 is the level of interpretation. Biblical interpretation is also known as hermeneutics.

So hop up to Level 2 and ask what principles/truths exist in the story. Let's consider, for example, the story of the Parting of the Red Sea (Exodus 14). I don't imagine God will grant you the ability to part a body of water anytime soon. But what are the truths and principles of this story? We see that God protects his people, his word triumphs against his enemies, and so on.

To interpret the author's meaning, never forget that the passage is part of a context (a.k.a setting). The context is the "neighborhood" around the passage and gives it meaning and significance. The context may be the verse, section, book, the Bible, or history. You can answer most of your questions when you study the context. Look at the verses that come before and after. What is the book about? When does it occur? What is its cultural background? How does your passage fit into the logical argument of the book? If you can, do a little research on the issues facing the audience. This is where a study Bible can be extremely helpful.

Your Bible probably has a list of cross-references somewhere on the page. Look at the cross-references related to your passage to see if the other verses help you understand the one you have in front of you.

You must always ask, *Is this passage only for a specific time or audience, or does it also refer to us?*

As you contemplate the passage and consult other resources and people, avoid jumping to unusual interpretations. Run your thoughts by a learned person, such as a pastor or Bible teacher.

THE THIRD LEVEL: THE APPLICATION OF THE PRINCIPLES/TRUTHS

Don't try to wrangle an application from each speck in the verse. That's where things can go off the rails. Stick with simplicity. What's the point of the verse or paragraph? What truths or principles does it surface? How can you obey or follow those in your life situations?

Returning to the Red Sea story, we saw that it contained some principles. One is that God protects his people, a consistent theme in the Bible. An application of this is that you can have faith and peace when you're in a challenging situation, knowing that God is in control and will look out for you. In prayer, remind God of this and tell him you trust that he will keep his word. God loves to hear you say that. A symptom of trust is your sense of peace.

QUESTIONS THAT WILL HELP YOU APPLY THE WORD RIGHTLY

1. Does this verse/passage give you principles by which to live?
2. Is this command for you to obey?
3. Is this principle for a specific time and situation, but not for you today?
4. Should you follow this character's example?

5. Does this truth give you something to do or something to believe?

6. Does this passage show you what sins and mistakes to avoid?

7. Does this passage give you promises from God that you can claim?

8. Does this passage give you new insight regarding God?

9. Does this truth give you new insight into your identity and what God wants from you?

10. How does this truth affect your behavior toward fellow believers? To unbelievers? To evil forces?

11. What specific things must you do or change to successfully live out this principle?

EXAMPLE FOR PRACTICE

Choose some passages from the OT and NT to practice working through the three levels. For interest and variety, try drawing your passages from Leviticus, Jeremiah, Matthew, and Revelation.

PARTING THOUGHTS

When you apply Scripture rightly, you produce spiritual fruit. People can sense the Spirit in you by changes in your attitude, behavior, and speech. For example, someone growing in the Lord, being convicted by the word, and choosing to live it, will begin to display more kindness toward others. She'll have more patience. She'll gradually see where she is being gossipy and critical and will start to be more constructive in her thoughts and speech.

Those are the kinds of things that the Holy Spirit is looking for from you. It's great that you can win at Bible trivia, but that's not the end goal. Plus, it can lead to pride. You want to see the word of God saturating your heart. You want the Holy Spirit to spark you to produce fruit in keeping with righteousness. Such fruit will glorify God and be winsome to the world. People gravitate to a person who is winsome and humble. That's how we reach the world.

Awake from Bible Slumber *should ultimately increase your desire for God and His glory. It should produce holiness. And it should help produce a winsomeness that will draw others to their Creator. That's what I want most from this book.*

Part Five
The Story Arc of the Bible

The Story Arc of the Bible

The first step toward gaining a better grasp of the Bible is to understand the big picture. What's going on, and how do the pieces fit in? Get a handle on the overview, and the details will start to fall into place.

This chapter will give you a "scenic tour" of the Bible, putting its events in perspective and order. I'll use a few maps and charts to make it more understandable. And I'll put the Bible books in context for you. I'll include information on the Intertestamental Period to weave the two testaments together.

First, let's look at the books of the Old Testament. The 39 books fall in three categories: History, Poetry (Wisdom Books), and Prophecy. There are seventeen books of history, five of poetry, and seventeen of prophecy.

THE OLD TESTAMENT

HISTORY	POETRY	PROPHECY
PENTATEUCH		MAJOR PROPHETS
GENESIS	JOB	ISAIAH
EXODUS	PSALMS	JEREMIAH
LEVITICUS	PROVERBS	LAMENTATIONS
NUMBERS	ECCLESIASTES	EZEKIEL
DEUTERONOMY	SONG OF SONGS	DANIEL
OTHER HISTORICAL		MINOR PROPHETS
JOSHUA		HOSEA
JUDGES		JOEL
RUTH		AMOS
1 SAMUEL		OBADIAH
2 SAMUEL		JONAH
1 KINGS		MICAH
2 KINGS		NAHUM
1 CHRONICLES		HABAKKUK
2 CHRONICLES		ZEPHANIAH
EZRA		HAGGAI
NEHEMIAH		ZECHARIAH
ESTHER		MALACHI

CREATION AND REBELLION

Genesis means "beginning," and that's what we see as the Bible gets underway. God created the heavens and the earth. He created angelic beings and his ultimate work, humanity. God is perfectly complete in himself and does not "need" anything. Still, as Bono said, *It's a mind-blowing concept that the God who created the Universe might be looking for company, a real relationship with people.*

God placed the first man and woman, Adam and Eve, in the Garden of Eden. The garden was a paradise of beauty and bounty. Tradition says it was somewhere in the Middle East, perhaps in modern Iraq. Later events would significantly change the earth's topography; you won't find the original apple tree.

We want more information on the creation, but the purpose of Genesis 1-2 is to establish God's creative work and sovereignty over what he made. God made humanity in his image, able to sense significance and to reason morally, and he gave them a stewardship: To tend and care for creation on behalf of the Creator.

In the garden, God gave the humans abundant plants and trees to eat. Only one tree was off limits: The Tree of the Knowledge of Good and Evil. God told Adam that they would surely die the day (i.e., the moment) they ate it. But every other tree was edible, so they had plenty of options. How ironic that they were tempted (tormented?) by the one forbidden fruit.

A severe attack on creation came next. In Genesis 3, a serpent, possessed by Satan, tempted Eve and Adam and tricked them into following his will. He gave the age-old temptation: *Do you want to know what God knows? Disobey him and choose the forbidden fruit*. The Hebrew text makes it clear that Satan directly defied what God said. God had said, *Dying, you will die*, but Satan said, *Dying, you will NOT die*. Adam and Eve, God is holding things back from you. Defy him and find out what he knows. Your choice will be the be-all/end-all for you because you will know what God knows and become like him.

They bit on the temptation; they ate the fruit (the Bible doesn't say it's an apple). And they immediately died spiritually; disobedience severed their relationship with God. Rebellion vaporized their innocence, and they'd later die physically. Their choice caused death to enter the world.

God had the right and the power to vaporize Adam and Eve immediately. In his grace, though, he sought them out. In mercy, God removed them from the garden so they would not eat of the Tree of Life and live forever in their sins.

And though they made fig leaf coverings to hide their vulnerability, God sacrificed an animal to give them longer-lasting leather coverings. Sin had entered the world, and the first physical death in history was an animal sacrifice to cover the two rebels.

Theologians say that when God made an appearance on the earth, it was the Second Member of the Trinity who came down. That's the one we would later know as Jesus. It's likely that Jesus himself, in a "pre-incarnate" appearance, sacrificed the animal for Adam and Eve. I wonder what was on his mind when he took a knife and carved it up?

Once Adam and Eve left the garden, things didn't improve. Their son Cain murdered his brother Abel. Rebellion and corruption eventually led to a great flood. After the flood, God told humans to multiply and fill the earth. Defying God once again, they joined together to live in one location. God's response was not to obliterate them but to give them multiple languages. That forced them to spread out across the earth.

Things seemed hopeless. By the end of Genesis 10, they were physically scattered around the earth; spiritually, they were sinners going their own way. They crafted idols to be their "gods." Humans were not the be-all/end-all, no matter what their pride might say. They would live, have good and bad moments, and die. They would always die. They were mortal and sinful, with no way out of their spiritual enslavement.

So God stepped in. Once again, he chose grace.

God reached down to Ur of the Chaldeans, a city known for its moon god worship, and called the son of a pagan priest to serve him. God told the chosen man, Abram, that he'd take him to a new place and make a great nation out of him. That nation did not exist at the time. In other words, God didn't choose his favorite empire. In his grace and sovereignty, the Almighty made a new one. Genesis 12:1-3 tells us that the LORD said to Abram,

> *Go from your country and your kindred and your father's house to the land*
> *that I will show you. And I will make of you a great nation, and I will bless*
> *you and make your name great, so that you will be a blessing. I will bless*
> *those who bless you, and him who dishonors you I will curse, and in you all*
> *the families of the earth shall be blessed.*

From the start, God intended to bless the world through Abram. God took him to a region which is the land bridge for three major continents. This is "Loop 1" of three OT loops. The loops will help you grasp the big picture of the OT.

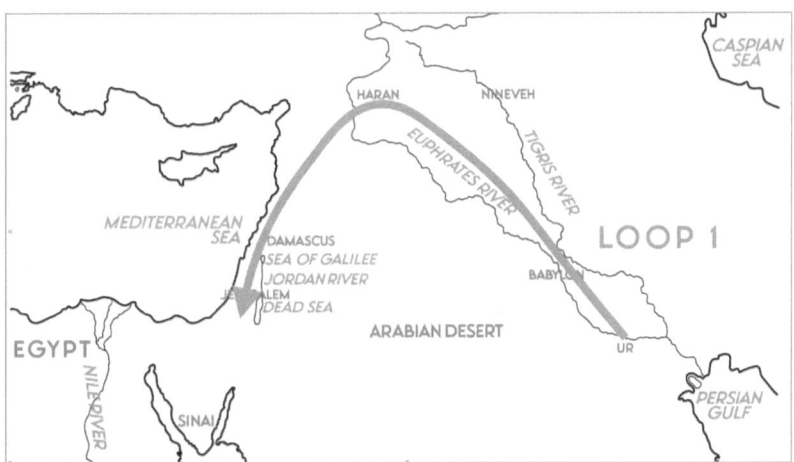

God changed Abram's name to Abraham and led him toward what we now call the Promised Land. On his part, Abraham had to choose to follow, even though he didn't know the destination. Abraham and his new nation would carry the light of salvation to reach the world with God's word. This new nation was not the be-all/end-all; it was not to be the final nation or the greatest nation. It was a tool for redemption. For God was going to create a chosen line that would lead to the one who would save the world from its sin problem. That man would restore humanity to its Creator.

They would know him as Jesus: "The Lord saves."

EGYPT THE INCUBATOR

The years went by, and Abraham had a son Isaac, who had a son Jacob, who had twelve sons and a daughter. Those twelve sons would be the forefathers of the tribes of Israel. The tribe of priests would be Levi (from whom Moses came). But Judah became the leading tribe. From Judah, the Messiah, the "Lion of Judah," would come. As we'll see later, he will become the be-all/end-all.

Jacob's favorite son was Joseph. The other brothers despised Joseph and sold him to a Midianite caravan heading to Egypt. Joseph was later imprisoned on false charges but eventually became second in command to Pharaoh, the king of Egypt. In prison, Joseph had dreamed that bountiful and lean years would come to Egypt. Once he became a royal official, he used his authority to store food for the nation. Famine hit the Promised Land of Canaan as well as Egypt. That caused Jacob to send his other sons to Egypt to ask for food. Jacob later joined them and was shocked and thrilled to see Joseph again. The book of Genesis ends with the Israelites in Egypt. It tells of the death of Joseph and how the Israelites kept his bones to return to the Promised Land someday.

The Israelites were few at the start, but as they stayed in Egypt for over 400 years, they became a mighty people in number and influence. They may have numbered as many as three million. At first, Pharaoh gave them favor. But as time passed, the succeeding kings "knew not Joseph" and, out of fear, oppressed the Israelites. The more the Israelites complained, the worse it became. Finally, the situation became intolerable, and the Israelites cried for deliverance.

And God answered. He raised a man called Moses. Moses was not to be the be-all/end-all, but he was significant.

Loop 2 takes the chosen people down to Egypt and eventually back again. Joshua will lead them into the Promised Land, and they will settle into tribal territories. Later, they'll have a series of kings.

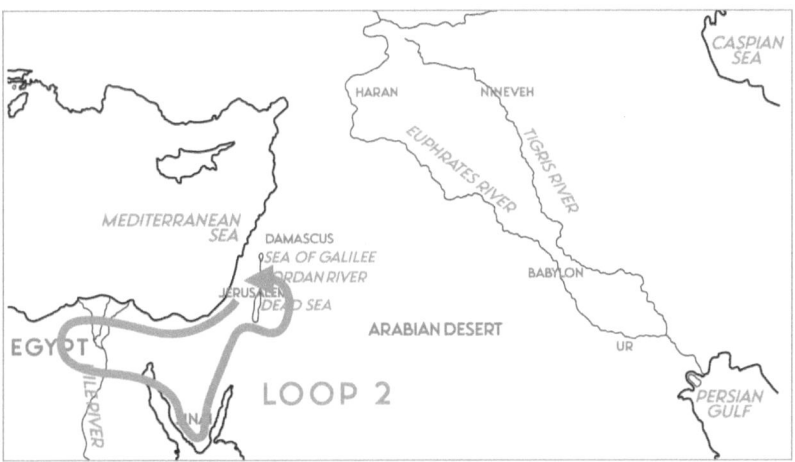

It turned out that God intended Egypt to be the "incubator" for raising the nation of Israel. But once Israel was fully grown and suffocating from oppression, it was time for her to experience a new message: Liberation—freedom through divine salvation.

God called Moses to lead the Israelites out of Egypt. The people thought they were dead when the army of Pharaoh chased them to the banks of the Red Sea, but God empowered Moses to split the sea so that they could march through it on dry land. When the army of Egypt tried to follow, the water rose and drowned them. The Red Sea experience would become a legendary story and a picture of the deliverance from sin and death that Christ would provide through his death and resurrection. Later, believers would realize that the two great examples of God's redeeming power (after creation itself) were the deliverance through the Red Sea in the Old Testament and the resurrection of Christ in the New.

Exodus comes from the Greek for "the way out." The book tells of the travail in Egypt, Moses confronting Pharaoh, and Moses leading the nation through the Red Sea to Sinai.

THE GIVING OF THE MOSAIC LAW

After going through the Red Sea, the Israelites began to head toward the Promised Land. They stopped at Mount Sinai, where God gave them a law filled with his righteous requirements. Because God revealed the Law to Moses, who delivered it to the people, it is often called the Mosaic Law. The Ten Commandments were the centerpiece of the Law, but there were 613 total commandments. They covered moral, civil, and ceremonial issues. The extensive system of sacrifices taught the Israelites that God was holy and demanded atonement for their sins.

The Law told the Israelites how to honor God in the Promised Land, but they could not fully keep it as sinners. The Law was not the be-all/end-all. It taught people about holiness and allowed them to display holy obedience, but it could not save the human soul. It helped the Israelites honor God until the Redeemer could come to earth and, on the cross, atone for humanity's sins. God would graciously give his righteousness to those who would receive his sacrifice by faith, not frail human works.

Romans 8:1-4 explains:

There is therefore now no condemnation for those who are in Christ Jesus. For the Law of the Spirit of life has set you free in Christ Jesus from the Law of sin and death. For God has done what the [Mosaic] law, weakened by the flesh, could not do. By sending his own Son in the likeness of sinful flesh and for sin, he condemned sin in the flesh, in order that the righteous require-

ment of the Law might be fulfilled in us, who walk not according to the flesh but according to the Spirit.

Through the Law, Moses taught the people to distinguish between clean and unclean. That would be important when they entered the Promised Land; the Law would keep them from socializing with pagans who did not honor God or his ways.

You'll see the giving of the Law in the last part of Exodus and throughout the book of Leviticus. Leviticus means "of the Levites" (priests).

TAKING THE LONG WAY HOME

The trip from Egypt to Canaan should have taken a couple of weeks, but a major rebellious incident happened along the way. When the Israelites arrived at Kadesh Barnea at the southern border of the Promised Land, Moses sent twelve spies, one from each tribe, to go into Canaan and scout the land. When the spies returned, they reported that the land was quite fertile but filled with "giants." Ten of the twelve urged Israel to stay out. Two spies, Joshua and Caleb, said the people might be big, but God was bigger. Israel should trust and obey God and launch into the land.

Unfortunately, the Israelites listened to the majority of the spies. And because they refused to trust God, he condemned them to wander in the wilderness until that entire generation of adults died. What should have taken two weeks took forty years.

By the end of the forty years of wilderness wandering, the Israelites ended up on the east side of the Jordan River, across from Jericho. Moses reiterated the Law to the new generation. The Greek word *deuteronomos* means "Second Law." Yes, the book of Deuteronomy contains this part of the story. Moses repeated the Law, emphasizing that when Israel obeyed God in the land, he would bless them richly, but when they disobeyed, he would bring disaster. The curses were the exact opposite of the blessings; obedience would bring abundant rain, disobedience would bring drought, and so on. And this was the pattern for the rest of the nation's history. Alas, throughout their history, we'll see more disobedience than obedience.

After giving these messages, Moses died. He never entered the Promised Land. It was Joshua who led them across the Jordan River. The Jordan was at flood stage, and God parted it just as he did the Red Sea. The God who was with Israel coming out of Egypt was still with the people going into Canaan. The first half of the book of Joshua tells of the crossing of the Jordan and the conquering of the land. The second half describes the settling of the Twelve Tribes into their respective territories. Tribal territory was vital in Israel, and we'll see its significance even in the NT.

WHO ARE WE TO JUDGE

The book of Judges tells us that once they were in Canaan, the tribes settled into lives of unfaithfulness to God. They repeatedly broke their covenant with him. It was a time when everyone did what was right in his own eyes (Judges 21:25) instead of what God wanted. Jerusalem had yet to be conquered, and the people had no godly king. They would grow spiritually slack, and God would bring a foreign power to dominate and discipline them. The pain would cause the people to repent. God would then raise a leader to defeat the enemy and bring liberation, and the land would have peace. But the people would become rebellious again, and God would bring another round of discipline. This cycle happened over and over.

The leaders God called to defeat the enemies were called judges, hence the book's name. You've heard of some of them: Gideon, Deborah, and the mighty Samson. The book of Ruth takes place during the time of the Judges. Ruth was a foreigner who married a Jew and would become the great-grandmother of King

David and an ancestor of the Messiah himself. We see a glimpse of God's love for all nations in Ruth's story.

The last great judge was Samuel, who was also a prophet. In the book of 1 Samuel, we see him provide a measure of spiritual stability during this rocky period in Israel's history. But Samuel grew old, and his sons were wicked and unsuitable as leaders. The Israelites wanted a king to lead them, just as the other nations had. But God warned them through the prophet Samuel that the kings would bring oppression and severe taxation and that the people would regret having them. As the saying goes, *Be careful what you wish for.* God was already their king, so the solution was for Israel to stay in right relationship with him. They should obey the Law and trust their God. But Israel rejected God as their king. They demanded an earthly one. So God told Samuel to give them a king.

SO YOU GOT YOUR KINGS

Samuel delivered to Israel their king: Saul, a handsome and strapping man from the tribe of Benjamin, who was spiritually shallow. Saul tried to manipulate God but never fully worshiped him. As a result, God prepared a young man named David to succeed Saul. Saul was paranoid and tried to kill David, but God protected his chosen one. At the end of 1 Samuel, we see Saul lose a battle with the Philistines. As they press around him, he falls on his sword.

After Saul died, David became king of Judah and later all of Israel. He captured Jerusalem, which became known ever after as the City of David. We read of David's reign—the good and the bad —in 2 Samuel. David was a great and wise ruler. A warrior from the tribe of Judah, he was a fierce fighter and never lost a battle. He also loved God wholeheartedly, wrote songs and poetry dedicated to God, and cared for the human heart.

David was the best king that Old Testament Israel would ever have and the one by which all others would be measured. But he was not the be-all/end-all. He was a sinner, committing adultery with the beautiful Bathsheba and setting up the murder of her husband. God almost ended David's life in judgment. David stayed alive, but his kingdom was no longer at peace. The child of David and Bathsheba's illicit affair died. Later, though, Bathsheba conceived a son who would be the next king of Israel. His name was Solomon.

David was the pattern for the Messiah. Messiah comes from the Hebrew word *mashiach*, which means "anointed one." So does the Greek word *christos* in the New Testament. Messiah and Christ are the same—the great Anointed One of God. The Messiah would be the Son of David. He would rule the nations (Psalm 2; Revelation 19:11-16). The Anointed One would be the be-all/end-all.

The first half of 1 Kings tells us about Solomon's reign. His name means "peaceful." It comes from the Hebrew shalom, "peace," and King Solomon would be a man who would bring peace and prosperity to Israel. He achieved great wealth and built a temple, a palace, and administrative buildings. The temple was magnificent and took seven years to build. The Bible goes into great detail about the materials and construction process.

Solomon asked God for wisdom and was known worldwide for his insight and wealth. His book Proverbs is a classic collection of wise sayings. Near the end of his life, Solomon wrote Ecclesiastes as the thoughtful reflection of a man who had everything in life but still felt empty. He concluded by telling us to enjoy life but glorify God. God will call everything into account.

As great as Solomon was, however, he was not the be-all/end-all. He violated God's direct command to avoid pagan women (who did not worship God). Solomon had a thousand wives and royal mistresses. They turned his heart from God. Solomon also built a large chariot battle force in defiance of God's command not to do so. Although Solomon was a man of peace and wisdom, those qualities were insufficient. His sinful actions brought havoc to the nation that God called to reach the world with his word. In the process, Solomon exhausted the people and set them up for disaster.

During the era of Solomon, Israel reaches the height of its territory and influence. The nation had its best days. Until the Messiah would come, that is.

THE SPLIT OF THE KINGDOM

The second half of 1 Kings shows that things went downhill quickly after Solomon. His son Rehoboam was unwise. Solomon had exhausted the nation with his building projects. The people were taxed out. But Rehoboam intentionally made it tougher on them. The result was that his empire fractured. Under the leadership of Jeroboam, the ten northern tribes split from Rehoboam. They created their own worship center. They took the name Israel; from then on, the ten tribes were known as Israel, the Northern Kingdom, or Samaria. The Northern Kingdom never had a king that honored God. The kings were notoriously evil, especially the wicked Ahab and his queen, Jezebel.

The Southern Kingdom took the name Judah after its prominent tribe. Judah would progressively decline spiritually, but the nation did have several good kings, such as Hezekiah, Jehoshaphat, Asa, and Josiah. As a result, Judah lasted longer than Israel. The book of 2 Kings alternates the stories of the kings of Israel and Judah.

The Divided Kingdom era was the time of the prophets. Elijah and Elisha were prominent, but they weren't the only ones. Other prophets gave messages to the various kingdoms:

- The prophets to the Northern Kingdom (Israel) were Hosea and Amos.

- The prophets to Nineveh/Assyria were Jonah and Nahum.
- The prophets to the Southern Kingdom (Judah) were Isaiah, Jeremiah (who also wrote Lamentations), Joel, Micah, Nahum, Habakkuk, and Zephaniah.
- Obadiah prophesied to Edom.
- The prophets in Babylon during the exile were Ezekiel and Daniel.
- The post-exile prophets were Haggai, Zechariah, and Malachi. The OT came to an end with Malachi's prophecy around 432 BC.

The larger prophetic books are called the Major Prophets: Isaiah, Jeremiah, Lamentations, Ezekiel, and Daniel. The other twelve prophetic books are smaller and thus called the Minor Prophets. There's nothing minor about their messages, though.

Below is a map showing each prophet and his "audience."

THERE AND BACK AGAIN

God had warned Israel in Deuteronomy that spiritual rebellion would bring disaster. And so it happened. As Israel and Judah declined, they became more subject to the influence and power of the mightiest empires of the time. Assyria destroyed Israel as a nation in 722 BC and took most of its citizens captive to Assyria. Those "Ten Lost Tribes" never returned. A few Israelites were left in the land and intermarried with Assyrians, creating a mixed race known as Samaritans. The "full Jews" despised them. We'll see this in the New Testament; in John 4, Jesus has a legendary encounter with a Samaritan woman.

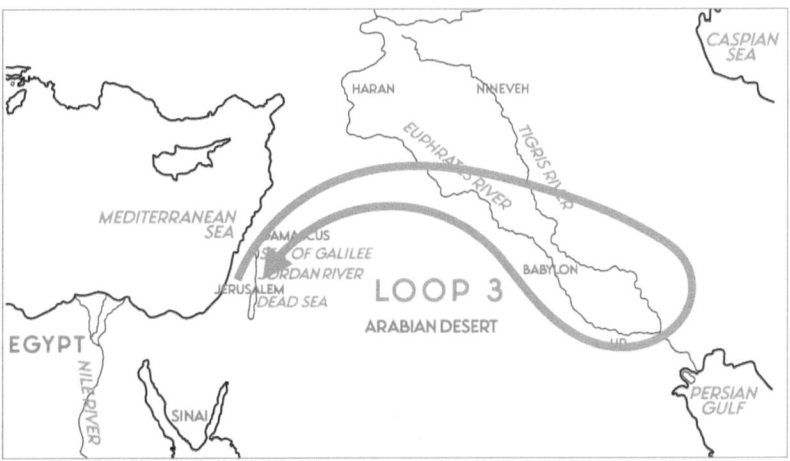

The Southern Kingdom of Judah was exiled to Babylonia in several stages, the final one in 586 BC under King Nebuchadnezzar of Babylon. As the Babylonians exiled the people of Judah, they also took the remaining items of value from the Temple of Solomon. Nebuchadnezzar used them in his palace debaucheries. The magnificent temple artifacts, which we had read so much about in earlier books, were now put to profane use. As for Nebuchadnezzar, he was the greatest king of his era, but God later humbled him. We see that in Daniel 4 when Nebuchadnezzar became a "man cow" for a few years.

The Babylonian Captivity of Judah lasted seventy years, one year for each year that Israel had neglected her Sabbath/rest years. Meanwhile, the Babylonian Empire declined, and the Persians conquered them in 539 BC. The Persian King Cyrus the Great then decreed that the Jews should return home and restore their temple.

Their homeland was in ruins, though. Nehemiah, the cupbearer to the Persian King Artaxerxes, oversaw the rebuilding of the walls of Jerusalem. The book of Nehemiah tells the story. The first part of the book of Ezra tells us about Zerubbabel and the temple's restoration. The second part takes place some sixty years later. In that section, Ezra the priest challenges the people to live according to the Law and to forsake marriage with foreign wives (who didn't worship the Lord). And because the people had focused on rebuilding their houses instead of the temple, the prophet Haggai called them to task.

During the Persian era, a plot arose to destroy the exiled Israelites. But they were saved when a beautiful Israelite named Esther became Queen of Persia. In their culture, the king could have killed her for approaching him without being summoned, but she bravely came to him and informed him of the plot. The king stopped the attempt at genocide, and Esther became a hero to her people. During this time, the term "Jew" began to be used for the Israelites. Mordecai, the guardian of Esther, was the first person in the Bible to be called by the name (Esther 2:5).

Judah was back home but exhausted from years of captivity and punishment for idolatry. Even though the nation had a calling from God, it seemed as if she had perpetually failed to live up to it. As God had warned them, they were not the be-all/end-all/greatest nation on earth. They could not even rule their own hearts by obeying God's Law. The only way they could have a spiritually thriving kingdom long-term would be to have the Messiah ruling it. He would not only have to give them a new kingdom; he would have to transform their hearts.

Only the Messiah, and his kingdom, could be the be-all/end-all.

The OT came to its conclusion around 432 BC. Judah was in her homeland, but her sin problem remained. She had learned a harsh lesson about idolatry through the disciplines and captivities of the OT era. Although she forsook idolatry, she began to live out the "letter of the Law" while neglecting its Author. In the NT, we'll find the Jews suffering from hypocritical and abusive leadership.

As the OT ended, the mighty Persian Empire was in control. And Judah was on probation.

CONNECTING THE OLD AND NEW TESTAMENTS

When we open the New Testament, we find that 400 years have passed since the end of the OT, the Persian Empire is nowhere to be seen, and the Roman Empire is in solid control. What happened?

The Jews had endured centuries of difficulty under the thumb of the Egyptians, Assyrians, Babylonians, and various other hostile nations. As the intertestamental period began, the Persians treated the Jews decently. The Persian King Cyrus sent them home to restore the temple, and afterward, they enjoyed relative religious freedom while under Persian rule.

Empires don't last, though. (Isn't it interesting how they are not the be-all/end-all?) The mighty Macedonian king Alexander the Great conquered Persia in 330 BC and also conquered Palestine. He allowed religious freedom for the Jews but spread Greek culture everywhere he could.

After Alexander's death at only 32, his empire split under the control of his four leading generals. Two of them —Ptolemy of

Egypt and Seleucus of Syria/Mesopotamia—founded dynasties that controlled Palestine. The Ptolemies were "ptolerant." In 198 BC, though, the Seleucids took over. The Seleucid ruler Antiochus IV Epiphanes was a revolting king. He overthrew the line of the priesthood and sacrificed unclean animals on the altar. Because he attempted to destroy the identity and religion of the Jews, they revolted against him, led by the Maccabean family. Judah won independence in 142 BC, but the period was known for continued Greek influence and civil war. In 63 BC, the Roman general Pompey stepped in and conquered Jerusalem. He killed the priests and entered the temple's Most Holy Place. The sacrilege was unforgivable to the Jews. Judea (formerly Judah) became a client kingdom of Rome. The hatred for Rome began. In 37 BC, Herod the Great became king of Israel and was declared "King of the Jews" by the Roman Senate.

The Roman Republic gradually became an empire. After the murder of Julius Caesar in 44 BC, his adopted son Octavian defeated Mark Antony and Queen Cleopatra of Egypt at the Battle of Actium in 31 BC. That opened the way for Octavian to become the first official emperor of Rome. He changed his name to Augustus Caesar, and the Roman Empire began in 27 BC.

THE NEW TESTAMENT: ALL HAIL THE KING

The dawn of the New Testament finds the Roman Empire fully entrenched in Palestine, with Herod the Great as their client king and Augustus the Caesar of Christ's birth. Tensions were high, and feelings were strong in Judea. The Jews wanted the Romans out, and they were ready for their Messiah to come as a conquering king to vanquish the Romans and establish a new, better empire after the order of David and Solomon. That explains why there was such a fevered reception for Jesus at the beginning of his public ministry. *The Messiah is here!* The problem was that the people—Jew and Gentile alike—were still sinners. That central issue had yet to be solved.

Galatians 4:4 tells us that in the fullness of time, when the time was right, God sent his son. The Roman Empire had severe issues, but on the positive side, the Romans created an environment that supported the proclamation of the Gospel. Well-built Roman roads covered the empire and enabled efficient travel. Greek became the common language, which made communication easier. And conditions were relatively peaceful under Roman rule.

In this cultural environment, Jesus came to the world via a lowly birth, in a humble manner, and prepared to sacrifice (Hebrews 10:5-10). Yet within a few decades, he'd be identified as the King of the Universe. In other words, he is the one who would be the be-all/end-all. The long-awaited Messsiah, the "Anointed One," the *christos* (Greek), the *christus* (Latin). Jesus the Christ. "Christ" was a title, not his last name.

Jeremiah 31:31-34 says, *Behold, the days are coming, declares the LORD, when I will make a new covenant with the house of Israel and the house of Judah, not like the covenant that I made with their fathers on the day when I took them by the hand to bring them out of the land of Egypt, my covenant that they broke, though I was their husband, declares the LORD. For this is the covenant that I will make with the house of Israel after those days, declares the LORD: I will put my law within them, and I will write it on their hearts. And I will be their God, and they shall be my people. And no longer shall each one teach his neighbor and each his brother, saying, 'Know the LORD,' for they shall all know me, from the least of them to the greatest, declares the LORD. For I will forgive their iniquity, and I will remember their sin no more.*

Testament is a translation of the Greek *diatheke*, which means "covenant." The New Testament is the story of the New Covenant coming in the Person of Jesus Christ to save us. Humans were not able to keep the Mosaic Law, the Old Covenant. Sin continued to reign in Israel. What was needed was a new covenant to forgive sin and bring righteousness. The New Testament tells how Jesus the Christ (the Messiah) came to do that. We find out that it required his sacrificial death for our sins. Once he accomplished that acceptable sacrifice, he was raised from the dead. His followers ventured forth to tell the good news around the Roman Empire.

The story of Jesus is told through four books called the "Gospels," written by individuals who had an eyewitness look at the ministry of Jesus. They give us four different views of Jesus as if looking at the same diamond from four angles, each seeing different facets. Matthew, Mark, and Luke used the common biographical approach. Because they see things similarly, they are called "Synoptic" Gospels. (Synoptic comes from the Greek "to see together.") The Apostle John took a different angle, beginning his book with the concept of Jesus as the "word." John bookends this description of Christ by stating at the end of the NT (Revelation 19:13), *[Jesus, the returning king] is clothed in a robe dipped in blood, and the name by which he is called is The Word of God.*

The books are called by the writers' names. Matthew was a former tax collector who wrote to Jews that Jesus had brought the Kingdom of God to earth as their promised Messiah ("Anointed One").

Mark was a protege of Peter who used Peter's input to write to what seems to be a Roman audience. It's a short, vivid, fast-moving book emphasizing Jesus's actions. His audience faces persecution, so Mark encourages them that Jesus was the Servant Messiah and Son of God who suffered and died as a ransom for sinners.

Luke was a Gentile physician and companion of the Apostle Paul, who wrote his gospel for educated Gentiles. He makes it clear that salvation is for Jews and Gentiles alike. Luke gives us the fullest account of Jesus's life. Luke wrote the book of Acts as the sequel to his Gospel.

The Apostle John was a close friend of Jesus and wrote the most unique of the four Gospels. It is more reflective and abstract. John includes materials not found in the other three Gospels. His goal is to convince his audience that Jesus is the Messiah, the Son of God, and they can have eternal life by believing in him.

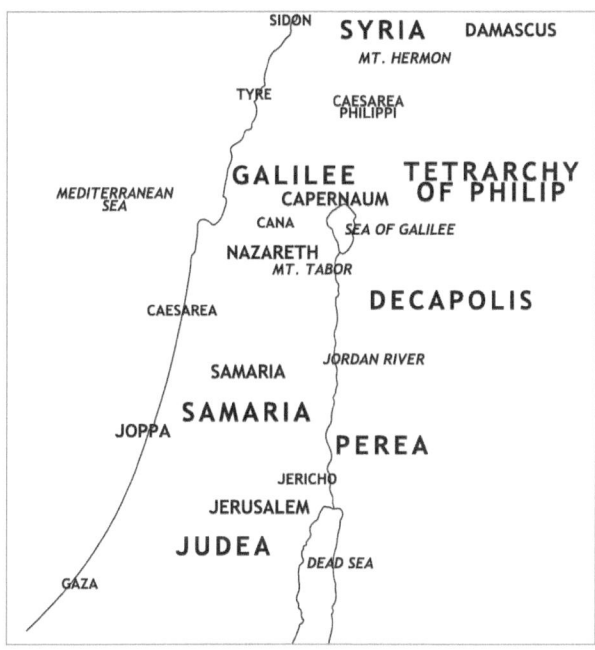

Jesus's family came from Nazareth in Galilee (northern Israel), but he was of the line of Judah. His father and mother headed south to their ancestral region to register in a census, and Jesus was born in Bethlehem, five miles south of Jerusalem. The birth location fulfilled the prophecy of Micah 5:2, given some 700 years earlier.

Herod the Great, the mighty king of the region, was quite jealous and alarmed when he heard of the arrival of the prophesied child. Herod ordered the murder of boys two and under around Bethlehem. Joseph and Mary escaped with their son Jesus to Egypt. With the death of Herod, the parents brought the boy to Nazareth. There he grew up. Sometime after Jesus was twelve, Joseph died.

The map below shows the general "loop" of his travels. Jesus was born in Bethlehem, was taken to Egypt as a young child, and several years later taken to Galilee. He primarily lived and ministered in Galilee. He did make forays to other areas; several times, he went south to Jerusalem. He was executed there in AD 33. For simplicity, this map does not show each trip to Jerusalem.

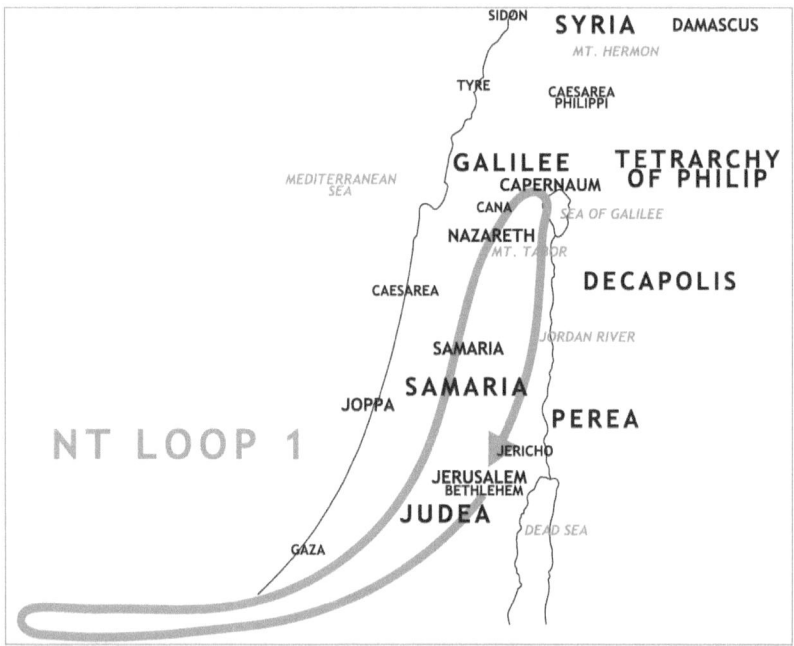

Jesus began his public ministry in his thirties. It started with his baptism by his cousin John, who is known as John the Baptist or John the Baptizer. (This John was not the one who wrote the book of John.)

As the ministry of Jesus picked up steam, thousands flocked to hear him and to see his miracles. They hoped that the Messiah had finally come, the one who would gather his forces and obliterate the Romans. The liberated people of Israel would be safe to sit peacefully under their vines and fig trees for the rest of their lives.

But his audience gradually realized that Jesus was building a different kind of kingdom, a spiritual realm of the heart that would transcend their current political situation. The disappointed and frustrated crowds began to dissipate. Some turned on Jesus. The religious and political leaders saw him as a threat and pushed to have him executed. But only the Romans could execute a criminal, so the Jewish leaders had to manufacture some kind of accusation sufficient to stir the Romans. And that's why the leaders told Pilate, *You're not a friend of Caesar*. To not be a friend of the emperor was to oppose him. In Pilate's mind, if that rumor got back to Rome, he would lose his position and possibly his life. He decided to order the torture and execution of Jesus.

The torture included scourging, a severe form of whipping that dug into the tissues of the back. The Romans specialized in a mode of execution known as crucifixion, a gruesome and agonizing way to die. The crucified one was nailed to a large wooden cross by the wrists and feet/ankles. He would be alive but would slump down and begin to suffocate. To breathe, he'd have to push up on the nails. This agony could last for hours or days. When the Romans were ready for the punished one to die, they broke his legs with a club. The person would slump down and suffocate.

But with Jesus, there's more to crucifixion than physical agony. During his hours on the cross, he bore the punishment for humanity's sins. His "once-for-all" sacrifice somehow atoned for the trillions of sins committed throughout human history.

And the Bible says that when Jesus accomplished the work of

bearing the punishment for our sins, he gave up his spirit and breathed his last. In keeping with prophecy (Psalm 34:20), the Romans did not have to break his legs. Jesus had been humiliated in the manner of his arrest, torture, and execution, but immediately upon death, his humiliation ceased. His body was placed in a rich man's tomb rather than a mass grave.

Many scholars believe Jesus died around 3:00 pm on Friday, April 3, AD 33. His body was in the tomb by sundown. Early that Sunday morning, several women went to the tomb to anoint the corpse with spices. But there was no corpse; he had risen from the grave! The family and followers cycled between disbelief, joy, and acceptance. Some had to see the risen body before they believed. But soon, all were convinced. The resurrection encouraged and empowered the disciples of Jesus. By the Day of Pentecost, when the Holy Spirit came upon them, they became a team unified by love and belief. They were fearless and assertive yet loving. They knew that all mankind needed to hear of the risen Jesus, his sacrifice for sins, and his conquering of death.

The Gospel books take us to Jesus's resurrection and some of his appearances afterward. That's where these books end. But we are blessed to have a sequel: The book of Acts, sometimes called "Luke Volume II."

Acts picks up the story with the resurrected Jesus ascending to heaven before his disciples. As he was about to ascend, his disciples asked him if God was about to restore the kingdom to Israel. But instead of directly answering them, Jesus told them it was not for them to know the time. And he added that they would receive the power of the Holy Spirit to testify about him worldwide. Days later, the Holy Spirit came down and filled them. Their confusion turned to conviction. Seeing the resurrected Christ and receiving the Holy Spirit, they came alive with hope and confidence. This motley little group began to spread the Gospel of Jesus's atoning death to all nations, tribes, and cultures.

They shared the message from Jerusalem to Judea, Samaria, Asia Minor (Turkey), Greece, and Rome. Jesus foretold this in Acts 1:8 before he ascended. The apostles had always shared the Gospel with the Jews but increasingly spoke to the Gentiles. As we saw in Genesis, God has a heart of compassion for all nations.

Acts begins in Jerusalem and ends in Rome, the capital of the empire. In general, the book's first half focuses on Peter's work with the Jews, and the second part shows Paul spreading the word through the Gentile world. Above all, Jesus is working through the Holy Spirit to grow his church.

Acts is a pivotal book, connecting the life and work of Jesus with the church experience that followed, which we also see in the Epistles. As opposition rose, the apostles fervently explained that the Gospel of Christ was not a new faith but an extension of what God had been doing over the centuries. In many ways, Acts is a bridge, uniting the calling of Abraham, the ministry of Jesus, and the mission of the church (see Acts 3:11-21).

Yet the risen Christ, and a Spirit-empowered church combining Jews and Gentiles, were new experiences to the believers. So in the decades following the Day of Pentecost, the church had to work out many issues, such as:

- What's our relationship with Judaism?
- How do we reach non-Jews?
- What place do Gentiles have in God's plan?
- What is the structure of the church?
- What is the structure of the leadership?
- What is the structure of the doctrine?
- What is the structure of the behavior?

The Spirit guided them through these questions, and the church quickly grew from a small group of 120 disciples to thousands. Today, in its broadest sense, the Body of Christ is said to number billions.

THE LETTERS, a.k.a. EPISTLES

The remainder of the Bible after Acts is a collection of "epistles." Epistle means "letter," and the epistles are letters written by various church leaders to churches and individuals around the Roman Empire. For example, in AD 57, while Paul was at Corinth, he wrote the believers in Rome a letter that we call Romans.

Each book has a historical and spiritual context. The writers encouraged the believers, rebuked sin and false doctrine, explained the faith, and challenged the flock to apply the truth lovingly. Persecution of believers was prevalent at the time, and the Epistles encouraged them to persevere because of the salvation they possessed and the glory to come. The map below shows the Mediterranean region with the cities related to the Epistles. Loop 2 represents the broad sweep of the Gospel toward the capital city of Rome. Paul made several journeys before his final voyage to Rome, but those "missionary journeys" are not shown in detail here.

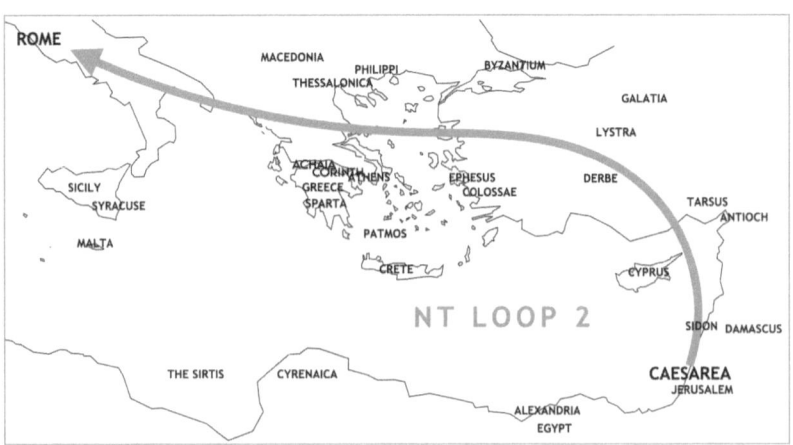

The last book of the New Testament is the epistle known as Revelation, thought to be written in AD 95 by the now elderly Apostle John, a friend of Jesus and caretaker of Jesus's mother after the crucifixion. John was living on the island of Patmos in an era of persecution. Tradition says that he was later martyred himself. In Revelation, he relates God's message of prophecy and encouragement: The forces of Satan will continue to fight the forces of God, but Satan has been defeated, and his time is short.

The book has a strong tone of glory and hope:

- Christ will strengthen his followers.
- Christ will prevail over our enemies.
- Christ will take us to eternal glory.

So the call of God to his people throughout the Epistles is to be faithful, knowing that the pain will end shortly but that the glory will endure forever.

In AD 33, the leaders in Jerusalem had manipulated the Romans into executing Jesus, but Rome brought the hammer down on the nation a generation later. In AD 70, the Roman General Titus destroyed Jerusalem. The Romans killed perhaps a million Jews, and many of the rest scattered throughout the empire. The dispersion is known as the *Diaspora*. In AD 132-136, the Bar-Kochba revolt led the Romans to implement a scorched-earth response that obliterated the remaining Judean society. Jews were scattered around the globe until the 20th century; many returned to the Promised Land when the modern nation of Israel was born in 1948.

First-century Jews saw a familiar sight: Just as Nebuchadnezzar's Babylonians had once carried the temple artifacts to Babylon, the Romans were now carrying them away to Rome. The items of the sacred temple were off once more to a pagan land.

Titus's victory was commemorated on the Arch of Titus in the Roman Forum. Carved into the arch is the scene of the Romans carrying the temple lampstand into Rome in a triumphal procession. You, the tourist, can see it on the Arch of Titus in Rome today. The tragedy is staggering. It did not have to happen. The people of Israel could have received their true king. Still, the earthly temple was not the be-all/end-all. It merely pictured the heavenly temple to come, as Revelation tells us. And God, in his grace, will bring Jews into his heavenly kingdom.

Here we are in the twenty-first century, suspended in time between the early church and the kingdom to come.

What's next for us?

THE STORY ARC OF THE BIBLE

Many are unaware that the Bible is an enormous story that clearly follows the Story Arc pattern. What do I mean by this? In the chapter on story, I explain how stories tend to follow a typical "arc." They will usually have these parts in some form:

- The status quo.
- An inciting incident.
- Rising action.
- An all-is-lost moment.
- Climax/resolution.
- Falling action.
- New status quo.

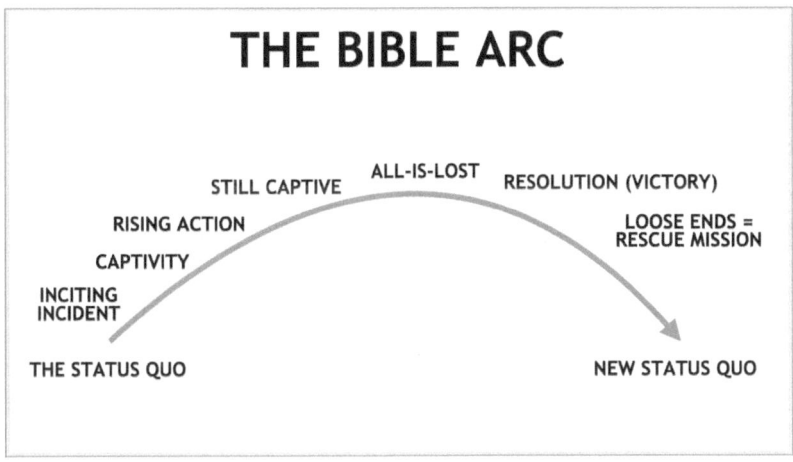

THE BIBLE ARC

ALL-IS-LOST

STILL CAPTIVE   RESOLUTION (VICTORY)

RISING ACTION   LOOSE ENDS =
                       RESCUE MISSION

CAPTIVITY

INCITING
INCIDENT

THE STATUS QUO   NEW STATUS QUO

The Bible begins (after creation) with Adam and Eve at peace in the Garden. When they yielded to the antagonist (the Serpent) and ate the fruit, we have, in dramatic terms, the inciting incident. The rising action is seen throughout the OT and in the Gospels as humanity's fate worsens. The all-is-lost moment is when Jesus is nailed to the cross. Satan appears to have won. But! It's not over! Jesus resolves the problem through his atoning death and resurrection. He defeats death and Satan, the one who brought it.

In some senses, the Bible afterward describes "falling action." This idea that our current experience is "falling action" should be highly motivating. It reminds us that our victory is won! It is certain. God has defeated our antagonist. Satan's doom is sure, and his power has diminished. It's only a matter of time before he is boiling in the Lake of Fire forever. With the sands of time running out, our job is to spread the word of rescue to the lost.

At some point, it will all be over. Our travails on earth will end, and we will have a new status quo—in glory, with our Creator. We'll have peace at last.

So the Bible itself is a giant story arc, displaying God's love for his creation and the extremes he took to rescue them when they lost the way. We see a glimpse of this in John's Revelation.

If you look carefully at the beginning and end of the Bible, you will find a remarkable contrast that ties the arc together. For if you compare the first three chapters of the Bible (Genesis 1-3) with the last three (Revelation 20-22), you'll discover this:

- In the beginning, God created the heavens and the earth (Gen 1:1). Christ is the Beginning and the End (Rev 21:6).
- God created the heavens and the earth (Gen 1:1). John saw a new heaven and a new earth (Rev 21:1).
- God created the universe and said, Let there be light (Gen 1:3). God gives the eternal city its light (Rev 21:23).
- In creation, the darkness he called *night* (Gen 1:5). There will be no night in the city (Rev 21:25).
- The gathered waters he called *seas* (Gen 1:10). In the new heaven, the sea is no more (Rev 21:1).
- God made the two great lights [the sun and moon] (Gen 1:16). The city does not need the sun or moon to shine on it (Rev 21:23).
- God made the stars of the heavens (Gen 1:16). Jesus is the bright morning star (Rev 22:16).
- Humans are to have dominion over the creatures of the earth (Gen 1:28). Humans will reign forever and ever (Rev 22:5).
- The Tree of Life is in the midst of the Garden of Eden (Gen 2:9). The Tree of Life is in the midst of the city (Rev 22:2). (Same tree?)
- A river watered the Garden of Eden (Gen 2:10). The river of the water of life flows from God's throne through the city (Rev 22:1).

- Disobedience in the Garden would bring certain death (Gen 2:17). In eternity, there will be no more death (Rev 21:4).
- A man will be united to his wife (Gen 2:23-25). The Lamb will unite with his bride (Rev 21:9-10).
- Humans were placed in a garden where sin entered (Gen 3:6-7). Humans will be placed in a city where sin is banished (Rev 21:27).
- The walk of God with man was interrupted by sin (Gen 3:8-10). The walk of God with man is resumed with the vanquishing of sin (Rev 21:3).
- The Serpent triumphed initially (Gen 3:13). The Lamb triumphs ultimately (Rev 20:10; 22:3).
- Disobedience brought curses into the world (Gen 3:14,17). The city contains nothing accursed (Rev 22:3).
- God would multiply the pain of rebellious humanity (Gen 3:16-17). In the city, there will be pain no more (Rev 21:4).
- God banished his people (Adam and Eve) from the paradise of the Garden of Eden (Gen 3:23-24). God's people will see his face in the city (Rev 22:4).
- The Garden of Eden was planted by God and lost by humans (Gen 2:8; 3:22-24). The city is prepared by God and enjoyed by humans forever (Rev 21:2; 22:5).

We glimpse the divine and human natures of Jesus (combined in one person!) through these bookend statements about him:

- *In the beginning God created* (Gen 1:1).
- *In the beginning was the Word . . . and the Word was God. . . . All things were made through him* (John 1:1-3).
- *The Word became flesh and dwelt among us* (John 1:14).
- *Then I saw heaven opened, and behold, a white horse! The one sitting on it is called Faithful and True, and in righteousness he*

judges and makes war. His eyes are like a flame of fire, and on his head are many diadems, and he has a name written that no one knows but himself. He is clothed in a robe dipped in blood, and the name by which he is called is The Word of God. And the armies of heaven, arrayed in fine linen, white and pure, were following him on white horses. From his mouth comes a sharp sword with which to strike down the nations, and he will rule them with a rod of iron. He will tread the winepress of the fury of the wrath of God the Almighty. On his robe and on his thigh he has a name written, King of kings and Lord of lords (Rev 19:11-16).

Creator. Word. Faithful. True. King. Lord. God. We've found our be-all/end-all.

At the end of Revelation, God invites anyone who is thirsty to come and *take the water of life without price* (22:17). A few verses later (22:20-21), we are blessed with words of massive encouragement as the Bible comes to its conclusion:

He who testifies to these things says, 'Surely I am coming soon.' Amen. Come, Lord Jesus! The grace of the Lord Jesus be with all. Amen.

God offers the gift of life to you. If you've never, by faith, received his eternal life, why not do so now? If you're reading this book, he is beckoning you to his kingdom of glory!

Part Six

A Summary Of Every Bible Book

A Summary Of Every Bible Book

G ENESIS

Genesis means "beginnings." It tells of the beginning of creation, humanity, the fall into sin, and spiritual hopelessness as humans continue to rebel against God. In grace, God creates the Jewish nation from nothing, founding a legacy that will lead to the one who will bring salvation. In Genesis 12, God chooses Abraham to be the father of the Jewish race. Genesis tells the story of the calling of Abraham and his descendants Isaac, Jacob, and Joseph (the Patriarchs), the forefathers of the Jewish race. Genesis ends with Jacob and his family in Egypt to escape the famine in the Promised Land.

EXODUS

Exodus begins with the Jewish people in Egypt 400 years later. The Egyptian king (Pharaoh) oppresses the Jews, and God calls Moses to lead the Jews out of slavery. Moses leads them through the Red Sea to Mount Sinai, where God gives him the laws that will be the foundation for the nation Israel. God also gives the blueprints for the "Tabernacle," a portable worship center and the place of his dwelling as the Jews journey home. He will be their God, and they his chosen nation.

LEVITICUS

While at Mount Sinai, as they prepare to move out toward the Promised Land, the Israelites receive further instruction from God on how to worship and honor him in the years ahead. God gives extensive detail regarding the Levitical priesthood, offerings, and sacrifices. The book emphasizes God's holiness and what he expects of this new nation, which he has formed to give his light to the world.

NUMBERS

The Israelites count their numbers (take a census) before leaving Sinai to head to the Promised Land. But on the journey, they continually complain and disobey. Fearful of the inhabitants of the Promised Land, the people of Israel refuse to enter the land. As a result, God has them wander in the wilderness for 40 years. During that time, the older generation dies out. The remainder end up on the east bank of the Jordan River, across from Jericho.

DEUTERONOMY

On the east bank of the Jordan, Moses reminds the new generation of their legacy and repeats the Law to them. (Deuteronomy means "Second Law.") He emphasizes that obedience to God will bring blessings untold to the nation but that disobedience will bring cursing. So he instructs them to obey God when they settle in the Promised Land. At the end of the book, Moses dies. He did not enter the Promised Land. Joshua becomes the leader of the Israelites.

JOSHUA

Joshua parts the swollen Jordan River and leads the Israelites through the river into the Promised Land. They divide and conquer the inhabitants, first in the south and then in the north. The book's second half describes the division of the land and the settling into tribal territories.

JUDGES

Judges takes the reader from Joshua's death to the brink of King Saul. After settling the land, the Israelites have no king. Everyone does what is right in his or her own eyes, and they go through a continual cycle of forgetting God, enduring harsh discipline, repenting, and being delivered by leaders known as judges.

RUTH

Ruth occurs during the time of the judges. Ruth, a Gentile, was loyal to her mother-in-law, Naomi, an Israelite. God led Ruth to a godly husband (Boaz), and she became an ancestor of King David and Jesus himself.

1 SAMUEL

The four books of Samuel and Kings tell the whole history of the monarchy in Israel. 1 Samuel takes the reader from the birth of Samuel to the death of Saul, the first king of Israel. Samuel was the last judge of the Israelites and also a prophet. He would anoint the first two kings of Israel. In Samuel's later years, the people of Israel demanded a king despite God's warning of the oppression that would follow. They get what they ask for--Saul, a striking man but of dubious character. Over time, Saul rejected God, and God rejected him as king. So God prepared a young man named David to be the next king. David honored Saul until his death and was a man after God's heart.

2 SAMUEL

David emerges victorious after a civil war in Israel following Saul's death and rises to the throne of Israel. David became the greatest king in Israel's history and the measuring rod for all kings who would follow him; that is, until his descendant, Jesus the Messiah, came to rule. God promised David the "Davidic Covenant" (2 Samuel 7); as long as a king sat on the throne of Israel, he would be a descendant of David. David established Jerusalem as his capital. David never lost a battle and conquered Israel's enemies, but he brought great trouble to his kingdom due to his affair with Bathsheba (who would become the mother of Solomon). David's life and kingdom would never be the same.

1 KINGS

1st and 2nd Kings are one literary work, later divided into two. In Deuteronomy, Moses told the Israelites what would happen if they obeyed or disobeyed God. In the Kings, we see the words of Moses come to fruition. In 1 Kings, David dies, Israel mourns, and Solomon overcomes his enemies to reign for 40 years. It was a time of peace and tremendous prosperity. Solomon oversaw the building of the temple and his palace complex. He amassed a vast fortune and was known worldwide for his wisdom. But he violated God's command against marrying pagan women, causing disruption in his empire. The kingdom reached its crest early in its history. Solomon rules over the largest territory of any king of Israel, but in 2 Kings, we see it fritter away.

2 KINGS

Because of his foolishness, Rehoboam, the son of Solomon, causes the nation to split into two. Rehoboam ruled the two southern tribes, and his empire became known as Judah, the Southern Kingdom. Jeroboam ruled the ten northern tribes, and his nation was known as the Northern Kingdom, Israel, or Samaria. The Northern Kingdom (Israel) would never have a godly king and would be destroyed before Judah, which did have several good ones. Still, both kingdoms would end up rebellious and be taken away in captivity: Israel to Assyria in 722 BC and Judah to Babylonia by King Nebuchadnezzar in 586 BC. (Judah's exile is also known as the Babylonian Captivity.) The Divided Kingdom period is also the time of the prophets in Israel/Judah, such as Elijah, Elisha, and Isaiah. Israel experienced the bitter taste of Moses's warnings realized.

1 CHRONICLES

Written by an unidentified priest, 1 Chronicles tells the story of a good ruler (King David) who rules as steward over God's covenant nation Israel. David conquers Israel's enemies to give the nation peace. He also establishes worship in Israel. With peace and spiritual obedience in the land, King Solomon (whose name means "peaceful") can build a great temple to the Lord in Jerusalem. 1 and 2 Chronicles appear to overlap the books of Samuel and Kings. The Chronicles relate similar events but focus more on spiritual themes. Samuel and Kings were written to encourage the exiled Jews. The Chronicles assure the restored

Jews that God still has a plan for them in keeping with their Davidic legacy. The Messiah, the "David to come," will indeed come for his people.

2 CHRONICLES

2 Chronicles continues the David-Solomon story. Solomon completed what David began. He led Israel in building the magnificent temple and established it as her place of spiritual service and repentance. As prophesied in Deuteronomy, if Israel obeys the Lord, she will have abundant blessing. Disobedience will bring disaster. Alas, after Solomon, the people fell away from the Lord. The kingdom split into the Northern Kingdom of Israel and the Southern Kingdom of Judah. The author describes the history and decline of Judah in chapters 10-36. Eventually, the Babylonians destroyed Jerusalem, forced the Judahites into exile, and carried the temple vessels to Babylon. How ironic and tragic. The book finishes on a hopeful note, however. King Cyrus of Persia tells the exiled Jews to return home and rebuild their temple. As a part of his covenant with Israel, God will move even the hearts of pagan kings to serve his will. Israel has a future, and God is in control.

EZRA

Ezra covers nearly a century of events. The book has two parts: Ezra Part 1 is chapters 1-6, the return of the exiles to Judah around 538-535 BC after Cyrus conquered Babylon. Zerubbabel leads the rebuilding of the temple in Jerusalem. The second part occurs nearly sixty years after the first, so you might be confused when you go from chapter 6 to chapter 7. Ezra Part 2 (chapters 7-10) describes the second return, led by the priest Ezra in 458 BC. Once the Jews are home, Ezra calls them to repent for marrying foreign women who don't worship the Lord.

. . .

NEHEMIAH

Nehemiah continues Ezra historically. Nehemiah, cup-bearer to the Persian King Artaxerxes, leads the third group of Jewish exiles home so that they can rebuild the broken walls of Jerusalem. They rebuild them in 52 days under intense opposition. Ezra reads the Law to the people in the town square, and they rejoice and repent. Although Nehemiah is not the last book in the OT, it records the final historical events of the OT. (Malachi was Nehemiah's contemporary.) The book shows how God protects his people and how they must remain faithful. Nehemiah himself was a godly man and a creative and decisive leader.

ESTHER

Esther is a beautiful Jewish girl who becomes queen of Persia and bravely saves her fellow Jews from slaughter. The Jews established the Feast of Purim to celebrate Israel's deliverance through Esther's noble courage and God's grace. God's fingerprints are all over the story, even though the book never mentions his name.

JOB

Job is an ancient story with a core question as old as the hills: *Why do the righteous suffer?* God allowed Satan to test Job by bringing him horrible pain and suffering. Job's three friends then show up and pontificate to Job. They wrongly thought God was punishing Job for sin, but Job stubbornly maintained his innocence. God finally confronts Job for his lack of trust but never explains the suffering. Job repents and expresses his faith in God's sovereign love. God issues a blistering rebuke to Job's friends and demands that they approach Job for forgiveness. At the end of the book, God abundantly restores Job's blessings.

Job is a thought-provoking book on many levels. It cautions us not to draw too many conclusions about what God is doing around us; his ways are inscrutable but just and loving. And it shows that the relationship between God and man is not a mere "transaction" (*Give me obedience, and I'll give you blessing*) because there are more forces at play. God may have purposes behind your difficulties, and Satan is always working to disrupt your trust relationship with God. Job eventually realizes that his trust must be in the person and character of God, not in his circumstances or "answers."

PSALMS

Psalms is a collection of 150 poems, approximately half by David. They are expressions of prayer and praise to God, drawn from a wide range of human emotion and experience. The Psalms emphasize God as the center of life, the sovereign Creator King who is good, just, and faithful. He is amazingly benevolent yet beyond our comprehension. He will reign forever, and all nations and individuals must yield to him. His covenant people Israel are to be a light to all nations.

Psalms is the songbook of God's people, starting with Israel and continuing with the church. The Psalms provide a platform for the transcendent praise of God coupled with a free expression of human emotion that ranges from ecstasy to agony. They contain utterances of thanksgiving, joy, sorrow, and pain. The Psalms, therefore, reflect the tensions found in living a mortal life given to the service of a sovereign God in a broken world.

PROVERBS

Proverbs is a collection of practical sayings on wise living, many of which were compiled by Solomon. The book emphasizes that knowledge comes from the fear of the Lord (1:7). The proverbs speak of the importance of wisdom, discretion, education, friendship, common sense, diligence, discipline, and the restraint of one's tongue. On the other hand, we must shun foolishness, displays of temper, quarrelsomeness, gossip, and sexual immorality. The book seems especially addressed to young men. As they live nobly, they should also marry wives of noble character (chapter 31). Wisdom will enable us to live happy and prosperous lives. It is encouraging to see from Proverbs that the spiritual life is not something lived in the clouds. It is visceral, vital, and practical. We must walk this earth in wisdom every day.

ECCLESIASTES

King Solomon experienced and examined all that life had to offer and realized that life apart from God is empty, unsatisfying, and meaningless. We should enjoy life, but only when we fear God and obey him do we find significance and satisfaction. Ecclesiastes is poetic and philosophical. As you meditate on the book, you'll look inward and contemplate the meaning of your own life.

SONG OF SOLOMON (or SONG OF SONGS)

Song of Songs, thought to be composed by Solomon, is a short collection of songs celebrating love and desire. Interpretations vary widely—some see it as the story arc of courtship and marriage, some as a collection of poems, and some as an allegory of the relationship between Christ and his church.

ISAIAH

Isaiah is massive in its scope and beauty. Isaiah prophesied over sixty years, during the reigns of five kings of Judah. He lived in the 700s BC. The book's backdrop is the decline of Israel, the ascension of Assyria, and the challenge of Judah to trust and obey the Lord. We see the full scope of God's relationship with his people. God is the sovereign Lord who judges and has overflowing compassion. God sends the prophet Isaiah to warn Israel of future judgment. Judah's sins will lead to her captivity, but God will redeem her. Isaiah gives a message of hope--the Messianic servant-king will come and *bear the sins of many*. Isaiah is a book of beautiful prose, poetry, and theological insight. The Suffering Servant/Compassion section (chapters 52-54) is one of the most moving passages in all of Scripture. Isaiah is the most frequently quoted prophet in the NT.

JEREMIAH

Jeremiah has the most words of any book in the Bible. The prophet Jeremiah's ministry went from 626 BC to at least 586 BC, a violent and stormy era. The smaller nations, including Judah, were caught in the crossfire of the empires. Assyria was destroyed in 612 BC, and Babylonia (under the great king Nebuchadnezzar) ascended. Nebuchadnezzar would exile Judah to Babylonia in 586. Before that, false prophets were telling Judah everything would be okay, so Jeremiah called them to account and condemned the nation's sins. The book is known for its prophetical judgments, but Jeremiah is the prophet who spoke of a new covenant that God would write on the hearts of his people. Divine wrath will be limited to seventy years for Judah. In his mercy, God would remember his covenants and restore Israel, demolishing the nations who once crushed her. Jeremiah's writing is mostly poetry, much of it lofty and memorable. We see in Jeremiah, a man who not only preached to the people but suffered their pain. Spiritual leaders are not immune to the sufferings of their people or that of humans in general.

· · ·

LAMENTATIONS

Lamentations is a set of five funeral poems written (probably) by Jeremiah, lamenting the destruction of Jerusalem by Babylon. Although mourning deeply over the city, the prophet knew God's judgment resulted from the people's sin. Jeremiah called the people to repentance and reminded them that God's compassion never fails. Great is his faithfulness (3:23)! As with the other prophets in the OT, the final word is hope, not despair. The book was to be read and sung in worship services to remind believers that God is the God of redemption, faithful to his people but requiring their repentance.

EZEKIEL

Ezekiel lives in Babylonia, where he had been exiled. Judah was in captivity in Babylon because she had profaned her temple and the name of God. His purpose for her was to be a holy light to the nations. After purifying her in judgment, God will restore her to holiness and glory. Redeemed, she will be a light to the nations. Those who believe in God will have eternal blessing. God purifies what was once defiled and will ultimately comfort his people. Much of the writing of Ezekiel is visionary and symbolic. Yet it is a highly-structured book; central to the book is the Babylonian destruction of Jerusalem in 586 BC, with chapters 1-25 before it and 33-48 after.

DANIEL

The teenage Daniel and his friends are exiled to Babylon. They serve in the king's court but remain faithful to God. Daniel eventually becomes a high-ranking official in the Babylonian and Persian courts, giving wisdom, interpretation of dreams, and prophetic visions about God's plan. Daniel's prophecies are accurate and tantalizing.

· · ·

HOSEA

Hosea was written in the final days of the Northern Kingdom before the Assyrians carried her away into captivity. God told Hosea to marry a woman who was, or became, a prostitute. Her unfaithfulness mirrored Israel's unfaithfulness to God. But Hosea's compassion for her showed God's relentless love for his people Israel, whom he regarded as his bride. God desired her repentance.

JOEL

Joel said that God's judgment of a terrible locust plague on Judah was like the coming Day of the Lord when God would judge all nations. Joel calls for repentance and promises that God will pour his Spirit on all flesh one day. (Peter quotes Joel 2 to the people of Jerusalem on the Day of Pentecost, after the ascension of Christ: "The Holy Spirit is now poured out!")

AMOS

Amos was a shepherd from Judah who prophesied to the Northern Kingdom of Israel in the mid-700s BC. Israel was enjoying a resurgence but was idolatrous, corrupt, and oppressive. She had experienced the kindness of God, but would not lavish it on others. So Amos rebuked her: *But let justice roll down like waters, and righteousness like an ever-flowing stream* (5:24). Amos tells Israel that God's patience has run out and he will soon call the pagan Assyrians to take her captive (in 722 BC). Yet one day, God would restore Israel to her land, and the Messiah would love and rule all nations.

· · ·

OBADIAH

The people of Edom were descended from Jacob's brother Esau and, therefore, the brothers of Judah. During the Babylonian attacks, Edom should have come to Judah's aid. Instead, Edom gloats over her superiority and is gleeful about the violent treatment of Judah. Obadiah says that God will return Edom's deeds on her own head (1:15). God will restore Israel but leave no survivor in Edom. Israel will possess Edom's land.

JONAH

The prophet Jonah despises the Assyrians, an empire known for its cruelty. When commanded by God to go and preach repentance to the capital city of Nineveh, Jonah hops on a ship headed in the opposite direction. A violent storm causes the crew to toss Jonah overboard, where he is rescued by a big fish (possibly a whale shark). Back on dry land, he heads to Nineveh and preaches repentance. He is bitterly disappointed when they repent! The book ends with God rebuking Jonah's attitude and expressing divine love for the great city of Nineveh (4:11). Jonah is a phenomenal study of the "mission heart of God."

MICAH

Micah was a prophet in Judah in the late 700s BC. He rebuked the leaders of Israel and Judah for their idolatry, corruption, and injustice. In God's judgment, two major empires will soon pounce on them: Assyria on Israel and Babylon on Judah. Yet, all is not doomed. The Lord will forgive and restore his people and rule in perfect justice. The greatest days are yet to come via the Messiah, whom Micah says will be born in Bethlehem (5:2). Micah calls God's people to just living: *He has told you, O man, what is good; and what does the LORD require of you but to do justice, and to love kindness, and to walk humbly with your God?* (6:8). It is God's design to bless the world with the Messiah and with justice and lovingkindness.

NAHUM

Nahum prophesies about Assyria perhaps one hundred years after Jonah, whose message of repentance had helped Assyria escape judgment. Nahum predicts the downfall of Nineveh as God's judgment for her cruelty. The prediction was fulfilled in 612 BC when Babylon conquered Assyria. God used the Babylonians to punish the brutal nation which once punished Israel.

HABAKKUK

Habakkuk, a prophet from Judah, pleads with God to stop the injustice and violence in Judah. But Habakkuk is surprised and disheartened to discover that God will use the even more violent Babylonians to judge Judah. Habakkuk complains to God. God responds that he will, in turn, deal with the Babylonians. Habakkuk then expresses his determination to trust God's unfailing love and sovereignty, even when God seems unresponsive.

ZEPHANIAH

Zephaniah was a prophet in Jerusalem during the reign of Josiah. He announces that the Day of the Lord will come when God will punish Judah and the nations for their idolatry and wickedness. And as sure, said Zephaniah, God will one day restore Israel to peace.

HAGGAI

Haggai was a contemporary of Zechariah. Haggai urged the

Jews who had returned from exile to stop rebuilding their houses and to focus on rebuilding the temple. He promised that God would fill the temple with his glory, as he had in the days of Solomon.

ZECHARIAH

Zechariah was a priest and prophet who returned from exile with Zerubbabel in 538 BC. A contemporary of Haggai, Zechariah gave a similar challenge to rebuild the temple. Zechariah's messages and visions bring encouragement to the people. He foretells many things about the Messiah (Christ), such as his coming in lowliness (6:12) and his betrayal for thirty pieces of silver (11:12-13). Zechariah predicts the siege of Jerusalem but balances that with prophecies about the Messianic age, including the return of the King and the annual pilgrimage to worship him in Jerusalem (14:16-21). Jerusalem will be secure and wholly holy. After years of captivity and difficulty, the Jews will rejoice that the God of history will remember and fulfill his covenant promises.

MALACHI

The final book in our OT is Malachi. He was probably a contemporary of Ezra and Nehemiah. After Nehemiah returned to Persia, the priests and leaders of the Jews grew lax in their worship and behavior. Malachi challenges them to clean up the corruption, reject marriage to idolaters, stop abusing the needy, and give their offerings to God. He calls them to covenant loyalty to God. Malachi warns them that *the great and awesome day of the Lord* is coming and that God will send *Elijah the prophet* to call them back to godliness lest the land be destroyed (4:5-6). The NT says the new Elijah would be John the Baptist (Luke 1:17; Matthew 11:13-14; 17:12-13; Mark 9:11-13). This conclusion of the OT helps to bridge the OT and NT.

NEW TESTAMENT

MATTHEW

The disciple Matthew, who has firsthand experience with Jesus, writes to a Jewish audience. He uses dozens of allusions to the Old Testament to show that Jesus has brought the Kingdom of God to earth as the promised Messiah ("Anointed One"). Jesus offers his Kingdom of salvation and peace to all, whether Jew or Gentile.

MARK

Writing to a Gentile and probably Roman audience, Mark produces a short, fast-moving, and vivid life of Christ. Mark emphasizes Jesus's actions. Mark is a protege of Peter and draws from Peter's experience. Peter saw firsthand the power, authority, and humble servanthood of Jesus. Because Mark wrote during a time of persecution, he focused on suffering, endurance, and discipleship. He presents Jesus as the Servant Messiah and Son of God who suffered and died as a ransom for sinners.

LUKE

Luke was a Gentile physician and companion of the Apostle Paul who wrote his Gospel for educated Gentiles, perhaps for those who attended synagogue but had not converted to Judaism. His writing is orderly, warm, and sensitive. Luke stresses salvation for Jews and Gentiles alike and shows particular concern for the mistreated. Many of his stories involve family and home. He uses eyewitness testimonies and gives us the most complete account of Jesus's life. Luke wrote both Luke and Acts to an official or patron named Theophilus. Acts is Luke Volume II.

. . .

JOHN

The Apostle John, a close friend of Jesus, writes the most unique of the four Gospels. The others use a similar approach and are called "Synoptic Gospels" (from the Greek "to see together"). John writes a more reflective Gospel that focuses on Jesus as the Christ, the Son of God. He includes details and discourses not found in the other Gospels. John gives stories of signs and miracles to convince his readers to *believe that Jesus is the Christ, the Son of God, and that by believing you may have life in his name* (John 20:31).

ACTS

Acts is Luke Volume II, as Luke shows how a motley group of confused disciples grow into a movement sweeping rapidly through the Roman Empire. As promised (Acts 1:8), the book begins in Jerusalem and ends in Rome, the empire's capital. The Gospel gradually transitions from its Jewish roots to the wide Gentile world. Acts is a pivotal book, connecting the life and work of Jesus with the church experience that followed (which we see in the Epistles).

In its first-century setting, Acts showed the historical foundations of the faith; in other words, it is not a new faith but an extension of a historical legacy. It clarified the Gospel to a world full of idolatry and legalism. It explained what made the church thrive, showing how the work of Jesus Christ continued through the followers he mentored, equipped, and empowered.

In general, the book's first part focuses on Peter's work with the Jews, and the second half shows Paul spreading the Gospel through the Gentile world. Above all, Jesus is working through the Holy Spirit to grow his church. Soon after Jesus ascends to heaven, the Holy Spirit comes down to fill/empower the believers

(Acts 2, the Day of Pentecost). Their confusion turns to conviction, and off they go.

ROMANS

In this magnificent letter to the believers in Rome, Paul systematically explains the Gospel of Salvation. All humans are sinners, but God made the one who is not sinful (Jesus Christ) to bear our sins. By his sacrifice, we can be declared righteous, redeemed, and restored—if, by faith, we receive his offer of salvation. Once we receive his gracious gift, we should yield our lives to him as "living sacrifices." Romans, in many ways, is the rock of Christian theology.

1 CORINTHIANS

Paul writes to the believers in Corinth during his Third Missionary Journey. They have become undisciplined, ungodly, and divided. He reprimands them, rebukes their errors, and rouses them to godly living. Paul emphasizes the Corinthians' need to grow in their holy character. Yet, despite the rebukes, Paul encourages them with magnificent passages on love (chapter 13), the resurrection of Christ, and eternal glory (chapter 15). 1 Corinthians is at once legendary, challenging, and inspiring. How blessed are we to know that *When the perishable puts on the imperishable, and the mortal puts on immortality, then shall come to pass the saying that is written: 'Death is swallowed up in victory'* (15:54).

2 CORINTHIANS

False teachers in Corinth were making untrue accusations against Paul and his apostolic authority, so he wrote an intensely personal letter to vindicate his character, challenge their faith, prompt them toward mature behavior, and urge them to discipline the false teachers.

GALATIANS

Paul heard that someone had misled the Galatian churches into believing in works-based salvation based upon obedience to the Mosaic Law. He writes them a blistering letter, condemning the false teachers and challenging the church to return to the Gospel of grace and Holy Spirit-prompted righteousness.

EPHESIANS

Paul writes a theological and practical classic to the believers in Ephesus. In the first half, Paul describes the greatness of our union with Christ as his body. The second half is about applying those principles in our daily walk as the redeemed. God saved us by grace alone, and we must love and serve one another and put on spiritual armor to fight our enemy, Satan.

PHILIPPIANS

Paul writes this letter of joy and encouragement to the believers in Philippi. He thanks them for their financial gift, encourages them to rejoice in all circumstances, and challenges them to stand firm when persecuted. He reminds the Philippians of Christ's humility and suffering on their behalf.

COLOSSIANS

Paul writes this letter to the church in the village of Colossae to remind them that Jesus Christ is supreme over all other powers and philosophies. The believer has been made alive in Christ and should live according to his virtues.

. . .

1 THESSALONIANS

In one of Paul's earliest letters, he writes the believers in Thessalonica, Greece. He had founded their church, and now they are being persecuted. He is grateful for their faith, love, endurance, and testimony. He encourages them to continue to please God. In every chapter of the book, Paul encourages the Thessalonians that the Lord will return for his people.

2 THESSALONIANS

Paul praises the Thessalonians for their faith under persecution and encourages them that the Lord has not yet returned (despite what false teachers have said). He encourages them to stand firm and not grow weary in doing good.

1 TIMOTHY

Timothy is a young leader in the church at Ephesus and a protege of Paul. Paul writes him a personal letter explaining how believers must behave in the church. Timothy must command and teach these things and be an example himself. To lead, he must have faith, purity, and courage.

2 TIMOTHY

Written from prison, this is Paul's last known letter. Paul encourages Timothy to follow his example, persevering through suffering and faithfully preaching the word—even when the world doesn't want it.

TITUS

Paul writes his protege Titus, the church leader on the island of Crete. Cretans are notorious for their rowdy behavior. Paul urges Titus to correct their false teaching and to challenge them to live godly, fruitful lives.

PHILEMON

Philemon is a short letter to Philemon by Paul, who had led Philemon's runaway slave Onesimus to Christ. Paul urges Philemon to receive his new brother Onesimus graciously.

HEBREWS

The author of Hebrews, who is unidentified, writes to Christians who have come out of Judaism. He reminds them that Christ is superior to everything, including creation, angels, Moses, the Mosaic Law, and the OT priests. The believers should therefore remain faithful to Christ and persevere through persecution. To shrink back will mean judgment.

JAMES

James, probably the half-brother of Jesus, reminds believers that they must do more than talk; true saving faith shows itself through perseverance and God-honoring actions.

1 PETER

Peter writes believers in Asia Minor (modern Turkiye/Turkey) and urges them to live in keeping with their holy calling. They suffer for Christ and must trust God and continue doing good. We can relate to Peter's promise: *And after you have suffered a little while, the God of all grace, who has called you to his eternal glory in Christ, will himself restore, confirm, strengthen, and establish you* (5:10).

. . .

2 PETER

Peter speaks to believers in general and says that we have the true words of God, not myths. God has given us everything we need for godliness. False teaching may creep in, but one day the earth and false teaching will dissolve, so live in faithfulness to Christ and await the day of glory.

1 JOHN

The Apostle John encourages fellow believers to abide in Christ's love, to believe God's testimony about Christ and have assurance in him, and to watch out for deceivers.

2 JOHN

In this short letter, the Apostle John warns a believing lady to abide in Christ's love, obey his commandments, and reject false teachers. (The lady may represent a church.)

3 JOHN

The Apostle John writes a short letter to Gaius, praising him for his support for traveling teachers. John also rebukes a rebellious troublemaker in the church.

JUDE

Jude was probably another half-brother of Jesus. Jude urges believers to contend for the faith, guarding against those who quietly bring rebellion and corruption into the church.

. . .

REVELATION

The final book of the Bible finds the Apostle John at the end of his life, addressing the churches of Asia during a time of intense persecution. God gives John prophecies to encourage and strengthen the believers through their difficult days. John urges them to stand fast against the works of Satan and a brutal empire, knowing that the Lord is battling for them and will return with glory for them. Before long, they will enter the eternal kingdom he will establish before their eyes.

Part Seven
A Theological Dictionary

A Theological Dictionary

T hese definitions are based on how the terms are used in biblical and theological discussions. Every attempt has been made to define them accurately and without bias.

ADOPTION God placing the believer in his family as a child, with all the rights and privileges of that position.

AGNOSTIC From the Greek for "no knowledge," it means "one who does not know if God exists." This person would say that he or she hasn't seen enough evidence to decide one way or the other.

AMILLENNIALISM The view that there will be no literal millennium (1,000-year earthly kingdom of Christ) before the end of the world.

ANGLICANISM A Christian tradition developed from the doctrines, liturgy, identity, and practices of the Church of England after the English Reformation.

ANTHROPOLOGICAL ARGUMENT From the Greek *anthropos*, "man." The nature of man (his morality, conscience, intellect, emotion, and will) means that there must have been a Creator with those qualities.

ANTICHRIST A term referring to anyone who denies that Jesus has come in genuine humanity. It is a popular term used to describe the final evil world ruler whom Scripture calls the Beast (Rev 13:1).

APOSTASY The abandonment of one's Christian faith.

ARMAGEDDON The climactic battle of history between the forces of God and Satan. From the Hebrew for "Mount Megiddo."

ARMINIANISM A doctrinal system formed by Jacobus Arminius (1560–1609) as a reaction to Calvinism. Believes that Jesus died for all humans, that God "elects" them to salvation when he looks ahead and sees that they will choose for him, that man has a free will but cannot save himself, that man cooperates with God in salvation, and that believers can lose their salvation.

ASCENSION The ascending of Jesus to heaven after the resurrection.

ASSURANCE The realization that the believer does possess eternal life.

ATHEIST From the Greek for "no God," means "one who does not believe in God."

ATONEMENT Has the idea of paying the price for a wrong and thus taking care of it. The work of Jesus Christ on the cross "atoned" for us by taking care of our sins; it "made amends" and reconciled God and man.

ATONEMENT, LIMITED Also called "definite" or "particular," this view emphasizes that Christ died only for the elect (those whom God has chosen to save). Part of Calvinism.

ATONEMENT, UNLIMITED The view that Christ died for everyone but that his death is effective only in those who believe the Gospel.

ATTRIBUTES OF GOD The characteristics of God that set him apart.

AUGUSTINIANISM "Saint" Augustine, the greatest theologian

of the ancient church, was a bishop in North Africa. Augustine believed that all men sinned in Adam's sin and that apart from God's grace, no one could be saved. God will choose some to be saved and will lead them to salvation. He strongly opposed Pelagianism.

BAPTISM The Christian sacrament or ordinance in which the believer is publicly recognized as being in the community of faith. The method of baptism varies and usually involves having the person dipped into water or having water applied to him by sprinkling or pouring.

BAPTISM OF THE SPIRIT The work of the Holy Spirit in joining the believer to the body of Christ (the universal church) at salvation.

BELIEVER One who has placed his faith in the work of Christ for salvation.

BIBLE The English word comes through Latin from the Greek word *biblion* (plural *biblia)*, meaning "book," "paper," or "scroll." The word stems from the papyrus plant from which the writing materials for ancient manuscripts were made. Eventually, *biblia* came to signify all the books of the Old and New Testaments.

BIBLIOLOGY The study of the doctrine of the Bible (its truthfulness, inspiration, etc.).

CALVINISM A doctrinal system formulated by John Calvin, a Swiss Reformer (1509-1564). Believes that man is totally incapable of saving himself, that God elects those who will be saved or else no one could be saved, that Christ died only for the chosen, that the elect will ultimately give in to the grace of God and be saved, and that those who are saved will persevere (not lose their salvation). It strongly emphasizes the sovereignty of God.

CANON OF SCRIPTURE The collection of books that survived certain tests and were therefore considered to be God's inspired word and thus authoritative.

CHASE, WILD GOOSE See Goose Chase, Wild.

CHURCH From the Greek *ekklesia*, means "an assembly of

people who are called together." The term may refer to a local church or to the universal church of God, which is every person in the world who has placed his or her faith in Christ as Savior.

CONGREGATIONAL A form of church government in which the authority is vested in the congregation as in Baptist, Evangelical Free, and independent churches. The voting system is, therefore, democratic.

CONSUBSTANTIATION The Lutheran view of the Lord's Supper, that the body and blood of Christ are present in the elements but that the elements do not change.

COSMOLOGICAL ARGUMENT An argument for the existence of God; the word comes from the Greek *kosmos*, "world." The world exists, so it must have a Maker, since something can't come from nothing.

COVENANT An agreement/contract between two parties. A bilateral (conditional) covenant is an agreement that is binding on both parties for its fulfillment. A unilateral (unconditional) covenant imposes an obligation on only one party.

CREATIONISM, IMMEDIATE The view that God's work in creation was without the use of secondary causes or processes. The earth, the universe, and man himself were brought into being instantaneously by the Creator.

CREATIONISM, PROGRESSIVE The view that God created the world, the universe, and man himself over a long period of time and through secondary causes that could have included evolution.

CREED An official statement of what one believes in. Three influential ones are the Apostles Creed, the Nicene Creed, and the Chalcedonian Creed.

CRUCIFIXION A form of execution in which the victim's hands and feet were nailed to a wooden cross. Death usually came by suffocation and could take hours or days.

DAY OF THE LORD A term that can be used for any judgment of God in history; it is used of God's judgment in the Tribulation period, the blessings in the millennial kingdom, and the entire period from the beginning of the Tribulation to the end of the Millennium.

DEACON A church officer/position; the deacon has spiritual maturity (1 Tim 3:8–13) and cares for the material needs of the congregation (Acts 6:1–6).

DEATH, SPIRITUAL Man's spiritual separation from God. He has no living fellowship with God and must be condemned to eternal judgment. From spiritual death came physical death.

DECREE OF GOD God's determination of what will come to pass. Can also refer to the command that comes from a decree.

DEISM The belief that although God exists, he is an impersonal God, uninterested in the world. He got it started but is not involved in it now.

DEITY The nature of God. Can also be used to refer to God Himself: "the Deity."

DEMONS Angels who fell with Lucifer when he rebelled against God. They continue to oppose God's work.

DEPRAVITY Man's sinfulness and inability to save himself before God.

DEVIL The highest ranking angel. Also known as Lucifer or Satan, who fell from prominence and is now the "slanderer" who accuses believers before God. Leads the attack against God and those who would follow God.

DICTATION THEORY The theory that God dictated the actual words of Scripture to the writers, who wrote them down in a passive, mechanical fashion.

DIVINITY The quality or state of being God (divine). Similar to "deity."

DOCTRINE A principle or position that is taught.

ECCLESIOLOGY The doctrine of the church, from the Greek *ekklesia* ("assembly"), the word for church. It includes what the Bible says about church structure and practice.

ELDER A New Testament church office, denoting someone

who is older and spiritually mature (1 Tim 3:1–7) and who provides spiritual leadership in the local assembly. The Greek word is *presbuteros*. The use of elder is generally in the plural in the NT.

ELECTION From the Greek "to pick out from," it refers to God's sovereign act of choosing some individuals for salvation.

ELOHIM A Hebrew name for God that emphasizes his strength, power, and superiority over all so-called gods. It is the Hebrew word for "God" that we see in the OT.

EPISCOPAL A form of church government in which the authority is vested in bishops, as in the Methodist, Episcopal, and Roman Catholic churches. From the Greek *episkopos*, "overseer" (bishop).

EPISCOPAL CHURCH A Protestant denomination representing the Anglican communion in the US; it also partners with the Church of England and the Scottish Episcopal Church.

ESCHATOLOGY The study of what the Bible says about the final events in the history of the world, from the Greek *eschatos* ("last").

EVANGELISM The effort to tell the Gospel to people so that they will commit to Jesus Christ as their Savior. From the Greek *eu*, "good," and *angelos*, "messenger."

EVOLUTION, ATHEISTIC An anti-supernatural approach to biological life origins, teaching that all life has evolved from a single cell through natural processes and chance over billions of years into the highly developed forms we see today.

EVOLUTION, THEISTIC A theological system that teaches that God guided the process of evolution as plants, animals, and the human race have gradually evolved from lower forms of life over millions of years.

EXEGESIS From the Greek *exegesis*, "to draw out" or "to explain"; the explaining of a passage of Scripture, especially by studying the original languages.

EXPIATION The concept that the death of Christ on the cross removed the wrath of God that was against us.

FALL OF MAN The historical event described in Genesis 3 in which Adam disobeyed God with the result that sin and death entered the human race (Rom 5:12).

FOREKNOWLEDGE Means "knowledge beforehand" and refers to God's prior knowledge of all things. Many relate it to God foreordaining those who will be saved.

FORGIVENESS The legal act of God in removing the charges against the sinner because atonement for the sins has been made.

FUNDAMENTALISM A conservative system of theology that holds to major fundamental beliefs of the faith, including the reality of the miracles of Christ, the virgin birth of Christ, the substitutionary atonement of Christ, the bodily resurrection of Christ, the physical return of Christ, and the inspiration and inerrancy of Scripture. Within fundamentalism are moderate and more extreme branches. The latter avoid fellowship with more liberal Christians.

GEHENNA The unseen place to which wicked souls go when they die. Comes from the Hinnom Valley, the area in Jerusalem where garbage was burned and the fires kept going.

GENTILE A person of a non-Jewish nation or faith.

GIFTS, SPIRITUAL Sovereignly given to believers by the Holy Spirit as a special ability to serve God and others. These gifts help to strengthen the church and evangelize the world.

GOOSE CHASE, WILD See Wild Goose Chase.

GOSPEL The message that Christ died for our sins and that we can therefore be saved from eternal judgment. The word means "good news."

GRACE God giving to man something wonderful that he does not deserve.

GRACE, COMMON God's unmerited (undeserved) favor to humanity in providing sunshine, rainfall, food, and clothing. It may also denote God's withholding judgment and restraining sin. It goes to all humanity in general.

GRACE, IRRESISTIBLE The Calvinist belief that when God elects someone to salvation, that person cannot ultimately reject the call.

GRACE, SPECIAL God's sovereign work in effectively calling some to salvation. It is for specific individuals.

GREAT WHITE THRONE JUDGMENT From Rev 20:11, the end-time judgment in which Christ condemns the world's unbelievers to the Lake of Fire (eternal torment).

HADES In the Bible, the invisible realm of the dead, both saved and lost. Most often used now as a synonym for hell (the place of judgment). From the Greek *a* + *idein*, "not seen."

HEAVEN The glorious dwelling place of God and the joyful abode of believers who have died.

HELL The place of torment for the wicked who have died.

HERMENEUTICS The study of how to correctly interpret the Bible.

HOPE The expectation of something great to come. In the Bible, it is not a wishing but a confidence, an assurance that it will happen.

HYPOSTATIC UNION Refers to the nature of Jesus Christ after he came to earth. In the Person of Jesus are two natures—divinity and humanity—in complete unity without mixture, change, division, or separation. He is both fully God and fully man, in one Person forever (he is not two persons). He has all the characteristics of man and all of the characteristics of God. This doctrine was clarified by the Council of Chalcedon and appears in the Chalcedonian Creed.

ILLUMINATION The ministry of the Holy Spirit in enlightening the believer, enabling him to understand the word of God.

IMMANENCE The contrast to transcendence. God condescends to enter into personal fellowship and live with those who have repented of their sins and trusted his Son for their salvation.

IMMENSITY OF GOD God's quality of transcendent greatness and supremacy in relation to the smaller size of angelic and human individuals.

IMMERSION The method of baptism in which the person is completely submerged in the water. Baptists especially practice this.

IMMINENT Generally means in theology that the return of Christ could happen at any time. It is "ready to take place," "impending."

IMMUTABILITY OF GOD Means "unable to mutate or change;" the fact that God cannot and does not change.

IMPECCABILITY The inability of Jesus Christ to sin.

IMPUTATION Means "to place on one's account," whether as a charge or a credit. The three biblical concepts of imputation are: the sin of Adam is charged to all humanity; the sin of all humanity is charged to Christ; Christ's righteousness is credited to all who believe on him.

INCARNATION Means "in flesh"; the eternal Son of God took to himself an additional nature, humanity, through the virgin birth (although he never ceased to be God).

INERRANCY The view that since the Scriptures are given by God, who has no falsehood and cannot lie, they tell the truth. His word is authoritative and trustworthy.

INSPIRATION The act of the Holy Spirit to superintend the writers of Scripture so that, while writing according to their own styles and personalities, they produced God's word. The Greek *theopneustos* (2 Tim 3:16) means "God-breathed." "Verbal plenary inspiration" means that the inspiration of Scripture extends to the actual words ("verbal") and to every part of the entire ("plenary") Bible.

INTERCESSION Prayer on behalf of another person.

INTINCTION In a communion service, the act of dipping the bread or wafer in the wine so that the person receives both elements simultaneously. Some do it to avoid having to drink out of a common cup.

JUDGMENT SEAT OF CHRIST The place and time when God gives eternal rewards to Christians (2 Cor 5:10). It seems to be a different judgment than the Great White Throne Judgment, which judges the unbelievers of history.

JUSTIFICATION The Greek means "to declare righteous." It is a legal act wherein God pronounces that the believing sinner has been credited with the righteousness of Jesus Christ. (Forgiveness takes away a negative, and justification adds a positive.)

KENOSIS From the Greek *kenoo* "to empty" (Phil 2:7), it refers to Christ emptying himself of his divine position and taking on human form in order to die. Does not mean that he stopped being God but that he put aside the privileges of being God. His life on earth was lived as a full human but one wholly dependent upon the Holy Spirit.

LAST DAYS The entire period from the first coming of Jesus (starting in Bethlehem) to his Second Coming. Often used for the last section of that period, when he is about to return and when judgments are taking place.

LIBERALISM An anti-supernatural approach to Christianity and the Bible that arose because of rationalism. Liberalism denied the miraculous element of the Scriptures, stressing the importance of reason; whatever disagreed with reason and science was rejected.

LITURGICAL A form of public worship structured with liturgy. "Liturgy" is ritual that includes music, praise, thanksgiving, remembrance, prayer, and repentance. Liturgical services typically read from every section of Scripture, recite a creed in unison, and have a sermon based on one of the Scripture readings.

LOGOS The most usual Greek term for "word" or "reason." Used also as a name for Jesus Christ, who is the personal expression of the thoughts of God to man (John 1:1, 14; Rev 19:13).

LORD The covenant name for God in his relationship with

Israel (Exod 6:2–3). "Lord" translates the Hebrew letters *YHWH,* usually read as "Yahweh." The name *YHWH* is probably derived from the Hebrew verb "to be," suggesting God is the eternally existing One. The word "Jehovah" ultimately comes from this. Because "Lord" can also mean "master," our Bibles translate Yahweh as LORD; that's why it's in small caps.

MEDIATOR An agent who mediates between two parties. Christ mediated salvation between God and the human race (1 Tim 2:5). As God and man, he represented both of us.

MESSIAH From the Hebrew word *mashiach,* "anointed one," and equivalent to the Greek word *christos* (also "anointed one"). It is a title of Jesus, designating him as the Anointed One of God who will be the great redeemer and leader of his people.

MILLENNIUM From the Latin "a thousand years," a period of one thousand years. Rev 20:4–6 says that Christ will reign on earth for a thousand years following his return to earth. There is debate about whether this is a literal reign on earth or whether it is symbolic for his rule over man. See "Amillennialism," "Premillennialism," and "Postmillennialism."

MOSAIC LAW The rule of God for Israel, given to Moses at Mount Sinai. Has three main parts: 1. Civil law, which legislated the social responsibilities with their neighbors; 2. Ceremonial law, which legislated Israel's worship life; 3. Moral law, found principally in the Ten Commandments, which identified God's timeless standards of right and wrong.

NATIVITY The birth of Jesus (from the Latin word for birth).

OMNIPOTENCE God is all powerful and can do anything that is consistent with his nature.

OMNIPRESENCE God is everywhere present, with his whole being, always.

OMNISCIENCE God knows all things, actual and possible, whether past, present, or future.

ONTOLOGICAL ARGUMENT An argument for the existence

of God: Since man can conceive of the idea of God (a perfect Being), God must exist.

ORDINANCE A God-ordained rite or symbol administered in the local church.

PARACLETE A title for the Holy Spirit; from the Greek for "one called alongside."

PARTIAL RAPTURE The view that not all believers but only those who are watching and waiting for Christ will be "raptured." Others may be raptured later.

PELAGIANISM Pelagius taught that every soul is created directly by God and that man is neither sinful nor holy. Man can choose freely to sin or do good and has the ability to take the initial steps of salvation by himself. God foresees the quality of lives people will live and predestines them accordingly.

PERSEVERANCE OF THE SAINTS The Calvinistic doctrine of the believer's security. Those whom Christ chose and died for are eternally secure in their salvation; they can never fall away or be lost once they are saved. Sometimes called "eternal security" and expressed by the phrase, "once saved, always saved."

PNEUMATOLOGY The doctrine of the Holy Spirit. From the Greek *pneuma*, "spirit, wind, breath."

POSTMILLENNIALISM The view that the world will become progressively better with the ultimate triumph of the Gospel. The world will then be "Christianized" for a millennial time, after which Christ will return. This view is influenced by one's perspective on current events.

POSTTRIBULATIONAL The belief that the church will be on earth during the Tribulation and will be raptured at the end of it.

POURING A method of baptism in which water is poured onto the head of the one being baptized.

PREDESTINATION God's planning, before time began, the destiny of his children, the elect.

PREMILLENNIALISM The belief that Christ will return

(Second Coming) and establish a 1,000-year kingdom on the earth. He returns before ("pre-") the Millennium.

PRESBYTERIAN A form of church government in which the authority is vested in a select group of elders (*presbuteroi*), as in Presbyterian and Reformed churches.

PRETRIBULATIONAL The belief that Christ will "rapture" the church before the Tribulation.

PRIESTHOOD OF BELIEVERS The belief that each Christian can relate directly to God without the intervention of a priest.

PROPHET A mediator or spokesman between God and men who received direct revelation from God, revealing God's will to man.

PROPITIATION The concept that the work of Christ on the cross satisfied the righteous demands of God and appeased his wrath.

PROTESTANT A Christian who is not of the Catholic or Eastern Orthodox church. Longer definition: It is a Christian who denies the universal authority of the Pope and affirms the Reformation principles of justification by faith alone, the priesthood of all believers, and the primacy of the Bible as the only source of revealed truth. The Protestant world is diverse, spanning the spectrum of liberal to conservative and unstructured to liturgical.

PROVIDENCE God's guidance and care. Sometimes capitalized to refer to God himself, who sustains and guides human destiny. For example, George Washington wrote *I hope we shall not forget that, to divine Providence is to be ascribed the Glory and the Praise.*

PURGATORY The belief held by Roman Catholics that all those who die at peace with the church but who are not perfect must undergo punishing and purifying suffering. After all sin is purged away, they are translated to heaven. The suffering can vary in time and intensity. Because the idea is based on a passage in the Apocrypha (2 Maccabees 12:39-45) and not in the OT or NT, it is rejected by Protestants.

RAPTURE When Christ returns in the air to grab the (universal) church and take it to heaven. This English term comes from the Latin word that translates the Greek *harpazo*, "to seize," which is used in 1 Thess 4:17 (*caught up together with them in the clouds to meet the Lord in the air*).

RECONCILIATION The concept that the atoning death of Christ restored the relationship between God and man (because God's just demands had been satisfied).

RECTOR A minister who serves as an administrative leader or priest. Primarily found in Anglican, Episcopal, and Catholic churches.

REDEMPTION Christ's atoning death bought us out of the slave market of sin, setting us spiritually free.

REGENERATION The work of the Holy Spirit which gives new life to the one who believes.

RESURRECTION The rising of Christ from the dead. Also, the rising again to life of all the human dead before the final judgment.

REVELATION Means "unveiling" and refers to the disclosure of truth from God to humanity that man could not otherwise know.

REVELATION, GENERAL The truths God has revealed about himself to all humanity generally through nature, providential control, and conscience.

REVELATION, PROGRESSIVE The gradual divine unveiling of truth throughout the ages until the completion of the Bible. Humans progressively knew more and more about God's plan.

REVELATION, SPECIAL The specific revelation God gave which was collected in the Scriptures.

SABBATH The Jewish day of rest (sundown Friday to sundown Saturday).

SACRAMENTS The term "sacrament" usually refers to a formal religious act commanded by Christ that is sacred as a sign or symbol of spiritual reality. Roman Catholics believe that seven sacraments confer sanctifying grace: Baptism, confirmation, confession, holy communion, holy orders, matrimony, and anointing the sick. Protestants tend to prefer the designation "ordinances" over sacraments, believing that the actions are commanded but do not confer any saving grace. Protestants generally hold to two ordinances: Baptism and the Lord's Supper. Some Protestant groups believe in additional sacraments such as footwashing, the holy kiss, and the *agape* (a fellowship meal connected with the Lord's Supper).

SALVATION Deliverance from the power and effects (punishment, death) of sin.

SANCTIFICATION From the Greek "to set apart," it is used of the process of making the believer holy. At salvation he is holy in his position before God, but in his daily walk he is supposed to grow in his personal holiness of life.

SATAN The word means "adversary"; Satan is a literal creature who once was a high ranking angel but fell from prominence as a result of his rebellion against God. He now is the leader of an innumerable host of fallen angels (demons) in his opposition to God and God's people. He is also known as the devil and Lucifer.

SECOND COMING OF CHRIST Refers to Christ's return to earth at the end of time. Also known as the "Second Advent."

SECURITY, ETERNAL See Perseverance of the Saints.

SEMI-PELAGIANISM The view that divine grace and human free will must work together for salvation, with human will taking the beginning step toward God. It believes that the effects of sin were more serious than Pelagianism represents. Roman Catholicism is Semi-Pelagian.

SIN Any defection from God's standards. The Greek term means "missing the mark" (of God's holiness).

SIN UNTO DEATH A sin that causes God to end a person's life prematurely.

SOTERIOLOGY From *soterion*, "salvation," and *logos*, "word"; hence, the study of the doctrine of salvation.

SOVEREIGNTY The supreme rulership of God. He owns everything and has the right to control what is his, and his divine purpose is always accomplished.

SPEAKING IN TONGUES The phenomenon in which a Christian spontaneously speaks a language other than the one that he usually speaks, without having to first learn the other language.

SPRINKLING A method of baptism in which water is sprinkled upon the individual's head.

SUBSTITUTIONARY ATONEMENT The sacrificing of Christ in the place of condemned sinners to satisfy God's holy and righteous judgments against sinners.

SYNOPTIC Refers to the gospels of Matthew, Mark, and Luke, because they record the life of Christ in a very similar manner. From the Greek "to see things together."

TELEOLOGICAL ARGUMENT From the Greek *telos*, "end." There is organization and harmony in the universe, so some intelligent mind must have planned and created it.

THEOLOGY The study of God. From the Greek *theos*, "God," and *logos*, "word." Normally used in a broad sense to signify the entire scope of Christian doctrines.

THEOPHANY A physical manifestation of God. Sometimes referred to as a Christophany, a theophany usually refers to an appearance of Christ in human form in the Old Testament (e.g., Gen 18; Judg 6).

TRANSCENDENCE God is separated from man and above man. He is holy and man is sinful; he is infinite and man is finite. God is "wholly other" than man.

TRANSUBSTANTIATION The Roman Catholic view of the Lord's Supper, which teaches that the elements are changed metaphysically into the body, blood, soul, and divinity of Jesus Christ while retaining the physical properties of bread and wine.

TRIBULATION When used as a technical term ("The Tribulation"), it refers to the future seven-year period of suffering and judgment described in Rev 6–19. Some see this as a symbolic time, others as a real period of time on the earth.

TRINITY While there is one God, there are three eternally distinct and equal persons in the Godhead, existing as Father, Son, and Holy Spirit. Each is distinct from the other, yet the three are united as one God. They all have the same nature. Think of Trinity as short for "Triunity."

UNION WITH CHRIST The idea that the believer is identified or joined with Christ, partaking in all his blessings.

UNIVERSAL CHURCH The combined group of all true Christians worldwide, from all local churches.

VICARIOUS Means "one taking the place of another," this term describes the death of Christ as substitutionary—in the place of sinners.

VIRGIN BIRTH Refers to Mary's miraculous conception of Christ through the power of the Holy Spirit, without any male participation. It technically is a "virgin conception." Not to be confused with the "immaculate conception," which is the Roman Catholic teaching that Mary herself was conceived without sin.

WESTMINSTER CONFESSION A statement of Calvinistic theology formulated at Westminster in London, England, in 1643–1646 by over 150 English and Scottish delegates.

WILD GOOSE CHASE See Chase, Wild Goose.

WORSHIP Reverence offered to God; can be done as a group or by an individual, in public or private. Means "ascribing worth to one who is worthy." Often refers to a specific service that seeks to do this.

Part Eight
The Incarcerated In The Bible

The Incarcerated In The Bible

D edicated to Chaplain Alicia Reeves and the offenders of the La Vista Correctional Facility, Pueblo, Colorado.

I have written this chapter to encourage and strengthen those of you who are incarcerated. Take this Scripture to heart:

> Not that I have already obtained this or am already perfect, but I press on to make it my own, because Christ Jesus has made me his own. Brothers, I do not consider that I have made it my own. But one thing I do: forgetting what lies behind and straining forward to what lies ahead, I press on toward the goal for the prize of the upward call of God in Christ Jesus.
> —The Apostle Paul, Philippians 3:12-14

Be encouraged that you may forget what lies behind you and that you may press toward a worthy goal. And please know that there is no shame in being incarcerated. You may have guilt and shame from what got you in there, but the fact that you are inside the walls of a jail or prison is not a shameful thing in itself. Many

of the greatest names in the kingdom of God have been incarcerated for one reason or another. If you are locked up, you follow a
long legacy of believers behind bars. And they stayed faithful to
him during their incarceration.

You can choose to join them in spirit by finding your identity
and purpose in God. And by living it out. Just because you're
incarcerated doesn't mean your life is over. God has a plan for you
—even in prison!

SPEAKING OF IDENTITY

God created the world good, and he created us in his image. We
are his children, made to rule creation with him. But when Satan
deceived Adam and Eve, he stole their innocence. By doing that,
he also stole their identity in God. And he stole yours and mine.
And instead of being rulers, we became slaves. Enslaved to things
like sin, addiction, and abuse from others.

Sin may have trashed your life, but you are not trash. You're
not worthless. God loved you enough to send his son to the earth
to be executed—yes, killed by the authorities—for your sins.
Receive Christ as your Savior, and you become the child of God.
God is reaching out to you and beckoning you to respond. He'll
purify your heart, as wounded as it might be.

As the child of the King, you have eternal value. Your life
means something—even in prison.

IT'S QUITE A CONTRAST

Take a look at life in prison versus life in Christ:

IN PRISON	IN CHRIST	SCRIPTURE
Not free	Free	Romans 8:1-2; Galatians 5:1; 1 Peter 2:16
Prison food	Wedding banquet of Christ	Revelation 19:9
Surrounded by the hopeless	Surrounded by the hopeful	Romans 15:12-13; Titus 1:2; 3:7; 1 Peter 1:3
Tortured identity	Child of God	Romans 8:16-17; Philippians 2:15; 1 John 3:1-2
Bound for nowhere	Bound for glory	2 Timothy 2:10; 1 Peter 4:13-14; 5:4,10
Stuck in a cell	Running a race with purpose	Philippians 2:14-16; 2 Timothy 4:7
Spiritual warfare	Satan incarcerated in the Lake of Fire forever	Revelation 20:10
Threat groups	Mightiest gang in the universe, forever	Matthew 13:39,41,49; Galatians 3:26; 2 Thessalonians 1:5-12; Revelation 12:7-9
Defeated	Victory	1 Corinthians 15:50-57
The Shot Caller	The Good Shepherd	John 10:11-18
Pain	No more pain	Revelation 21:4
Separated from loved ones	In the family of God	Romans 8:14-17; Ephesians 1:3-10,18
Not home	Home	Hebrews 11:16; Revelation 21:3

GOD'S PEOPLE HAVE BEEN INCARCERATED *A LOT*

You're not alone. Thousands have gone before you behind the bars. They kept their testimony and have been used by God. They are your eternal brothers and sisters, and you're in their family. If you're on God's side, you're a member of the team that will be victorious forever. No matter how dark it looks right now.

Their crimes, the accusations against them, and their incarcerations were different than yours, of course. But God was still in control, and he did not forget them. And he hasn't forgotten you.

It's astounding to think how many major figures in the history of the kingdom of God have been incarcerated. Here are a few:

- Joseph was a key member of Jacob's family who became the second-in-command for the king of Egypt. But before that, he was falsely accused and thrown into prison for years. See Genesis 39-42.
- The Israelites in Egypt in Exodus 1-2. Their 400 years in Egypt started well but ended with them being enslaved by the king of Egypt and forced to work to exhaustion. They cried for freedom and to go back to their homeland.
- The mighty Samson, Judges 16. He lost his strength by his foolishness and disobedience to God. He was imprisoned, and his eyes were gouged out.
- David was the great King of Israel and ancestor of Jesus Christ, who would both save and rule the world. David was pursued several times. King Saul tried to kill him, and so did David's son Absalom.
- The Northern Kingdom of Israel was led captive to Assyria in 722 BC and never returned.
- The Southern Kingdom of Judah was taken captive to Babylon in 586 BC. They weren't released for 70 years. (Jeremiah 13:19; 20:4.)
- According to tradition, the great prophet Isaiah died by being cut in half.
- Jeremiah was jailed in the court of the guard (Jeremiah 33:1). Tradition says that he was executed by stoning.
- King Zedekiah (Jeremiah 52:11) was forced to watch the execution of his sons, after which his eyes were gouged out. He was then bound in chains and taken to Babylon.
- Daniel and his friends (Daniel 3; Daniel 6). Daniel was a respected prophet who spoke to kings and foretold the works of God throughout time. The Bible never mentions a sin that he committed. Still, he was set up and placed in a blazing fire and a den of lions. He should

not have lived. But it shows that God can carry us through anything.

- John the Baptist was incarcerated for boldly calling out the king's sin. Eventually, he was beheaded in prison. He was the cousin of Jesus and baptized Jesus. (Matthew 4:12; 11:2; 14:3-12.)

- Jesus Christ was jailed and tortured by scourging and beating. The Romans scourged their prisoners by using a whip with leather thongs, with bone and metal embedded in the tips of the thongs. It would take the skin off the victim's back and even tear into the muscle. But crucifixion was worse. The Romans drove large nails like railroad spikes into the hands (or wrists) and ankles. Then they'd raise the cross and slam it into a hole. The weight of the body would smash into the nails. The victim would slump down and start to suffocate. He'd breathe again by pulling himself up—on the nails. Then he'd slump again. This cycle could go on for several days, so when the Romans were ready for him to die, they'd take a club and break his legs. He couldn't support his weight, so he'd slump down and suffocate. Jesus went through this for several hours while paying the price for your sins. He finally died by giving up his spirit. Is he worth our time and attention?

- Peter and the apostles (Acts 5). Peter was a leading apostle and friend of Jesus Christ. He and his comrades were imprisoned and beaten.

- Stephen was falsely accused, tried, and stoned to death (Acts 6-7).

- Christians were dragged out of their homes and imprisoned by Saul (Acts 8:3). He persecuted them to death. He put both men and women in prison (Acts 22:4). Ironically, the Lord Jesus Christ appeared to him, and he became a fervent evangelist named Paul. He helped establish the church throughout the Roman Empire and wrote some of our most important New Testament epistles.

- Peter was imprisoned again and watched by multiple guards (Acts 12).
- Paul and his companion Silas were beaten by the authorities and imprisoned (Acts 16). While they were praying and singing hymns, an earthquake damaged the jail. The jailer thought the prisoners had escaped, so he tried to kill himself. Paul and Silas stopped him and led him to Christ. The jailer took them home and cleansed their wounds. They baptized him and his family. In other words, the prisoner baptized the warden.
- Later, Paul experienced a series of incarcerations (Acts 22-28). He was jailed for two years. Some of it was house arrest, and some was protection from the mob that wanted to kill him. At night, he was taken out of Jerusalem to escape a team of assassins. In Rome, he was in light custody initially, a house arrest situation (Acts 28). But later, he would be imprisoned and executed there (2 Timothy 2:9). His final recorded words were *The Lord be with your spirit. Grace be with you* (2 Timothy 4:22). This is what your fellow prisoner wished for you as he faced execution.
- Christians throughout the centuries (Hebrews 11:36; 13:3; 1 Peter 4:12; Revelation 2:10).
- The disciples/apostles. Legend says that they were martyred for the faith in different ways. Peter, for example, was crucified upside down.

After Jesus ascended to heaven, untold thousands of believers have been incarcerated. Here are a few:

- The Scillitan Martyrs of North Africa, seven men and five women, who were incarcerated, tried, and executed in the second century.
- The reformer Jan Hus was imprisoned and burned at the stake in 1415.
- Martin Luther, German theologian and pastor who ignited the Reformation. Luther had to go into hiding for nearly a year because of threats on his life.
- In Oxford, England, the church leaders Thomas Cranmer, Hugh Latimer, and Nicholas Ridley were imprisoned and burned at the stake.
- John Bunyan, the English pastor who wrote *The Pilgrim's Progress*, was imprisoned for twelve years.
- Dietrich Bonhoeffer, the influential German pastor imprisoned by the Nazis during World War II. They executed him right before the war ended.
- Corrie ten Boom, arrested by the Nazis for hiding Jews during the Holocaust. The Nazis put her in the Ravensbrück concentration camp. She wrote her classic book, *The Hiding Place*, while imprisoned in the camp. Corrie saved the lives of an estimated 800 Jews. Her sister Betsie died in the camp; before she died, Betsie told Corrie, "There is no pit so deep that he [God] is not deeper still."
- Richard Wurmbrand, imprisoned and tortured by the Communists for 14 years and founder of *The Voice of the Martyrs*, a ministry to the persecuted around the world.
- Petr Jasek, a missionary imprisoned in the same cell with terrorists in Sudan.
- There have been more martyrs for the faith in the last 100 years than the rest of church history combined. I have worked with people imprisoned and tortured for their faithfulness to Christ. One of them, in Africa, took a rocket (not a bullet) through the leg. He was in pain

every day but stayed faithful. A man in Asia told me he was imprisoned and beaten eleven different times for his faith. He said that he was honored to serve Christ that way.

- Martin Luther King, Jr., the influential American pastor who wrote the landmark "Letters from Birmingham Jail." He was later assassinated but died a witness to the faithfulness, justice, and mercy of God.
- Colonel Ellis, a strong believer and a friend of mine, was locked up in an enemy prison camp for six years. He and his fellow prisoners were beaten and tortured. Some died.

WHERE DO YOU GO FROM HERE?

Just before he was executed, Paul considered his life situation:

For I am already being poured out as a drink offering, and the time of my departure has come. I have fought the good fight, I have finished the race, I have kept the faith. Henceforth there is laid up for me the crown of right-eousness, which the Lord, the righteous judge, will award to me on that day, and not only to me but also to all who have loved his appearing.
  —2 Timothy 4:6-8

As an apostle, Paul had suffered beatings, stonings, shipwrecks (at least four!), and countless other hardships. His body was a battered, useless mess. His emotions were stretched thin. His best life was not going to be on this earth. But he was about to find his best life with Christ in heaven.

It goes the same way for you and me. Our best life isn't on this earth. But in eternity, your incarceration will be a distant memory. Your prison term will be blotted out forever. Your "eternal lockup" is heaven, not prison. You are bound for a place without bars. It's a place where you'll be safe—forever.

Wouldn't it be awesome to consider yourself the child of God? To know that a crown will await you because you overcame life's hardships? It has happened to others and can happen to you. So stay in the spiritual race—don't give up on God, and don't give up on yourself.

*Do you realize that God has a plan for you **right now**? Could it be that he has something for you to do in prison? Why has he allowed you to be there?*

Can you trust in his strength to carry you through?

(For those who are not incarcerated—pray for God to give you people with whom to share this message.)

Conclusion

Blessed be the name of the LORD from this time forth and forevermore!
From the rising of the sun to its setting, the name of the LORD is to be praised!
—Psalm 113:2-3

Now that you've reached the end of the book, what do you do with what you've learned?

The first thing is to commit to being faithful to the Lord for the rest of your days. Faithfulness is not a given. Dr. Howard Hendricks told my class that only 2,930 people are mentioned by name in the Bible. In only 100 cases do we have enough information to know if the person finished well. Of those 100 cases, only one-third did. *Be one of those who finish well, not one who falls away.*

The battle for consistency is never-ending. Focus is hard to find. The cares of the world choke out the word. A major factor in faithfulness is choosing to spend time with God and his word daily. Most of us have to eat our three meals every day. So why do we fast from the word that spiritually nourishes and sustains us? Why do we make ourselves spiritually anemic?

Your time with God will have to become a habit. Experts on

habit (such as Charles Duhigg in *The Power of Habit*) tell us that for something to be a habit, there must be a "cue" or trigger. Find something that will trigger your time with God every day. What if you made your morning coffee and got with the Lord before you ate breakfast? Or, perhaps you can spend time with him during breakfast (unless you have kids!).

There are different approaches to daily time with God (a.k.a. "quiet time"). You can go through a Bible book and use the concepts of this book to help you better understand the daily passage. Or, go online and find a daily Bible reading program. There are an infinite amount of resources.

Don't fixate on covering a certain amount of time or a certain quantity of Scripture every day. Fixate on faithfulness. You want to leverage the power of spiritual compounding—a little a day will add up over time and reap great rewards!

And be at peace with the fact that your sense of closeness with God will come and go. God may even appear to "move away" for a while so that your faith will be anchored to his character, not your feelings. But he is always infinitely close to you.

I am convinced that you can understand the Bible! Sure, some parts are mysterious for all of us, but don't let that be an excuse not to try to grasp as much as you can. The big picture is especially knowable.

May God grant you commitment and clarity!

See you at the heavenly banquet!

Acknowledgments

For their impact in my life:

My wife Suzy, co-hiker on the up-down-up journey of life and ministry for decades.

My awesome daughter Summer Ploegman and her commitment to the future. The beloved Dr. Adam Ploegman, my favorite Cubbie.

Dallas Theological Seminary. Nine years later, I was a deeper and better man.

The late Professor Howard Hendricks, whose work on inductive Bible study ultimately affected millions. "Prof" led the way, and this book is one of countless results of his labor.

Dallas Seminary professors Allan P. Ross and Kenneth L. Barker, who showed me how to go so much deeper in the Bible. I stand in awe

Walk Thru the Bible Ministries, Norcross, Georgia. The impact of WTB in my life cannot be calculated. Thanks to Phil Tuttle, WTB President and comrade.

The Black Forest wildfire, a vivid reminder in my later years of what really matters in life. It destroyed all my books, but not my spirit or purpose.

∽

For their role in the development of this material:

The students of the Gilmer Christian Learning Center, Ellijay, Georgia.

The students of the Brookwood Christian Learning Center, Snellville, Georgia.

The family of Grace Fellowship Church, Snellville, Georgia. Especially the amazing Dr. Tyler Thigpen. Tyler, thanks for helping this concept to take wing in the hills of Georgia and Peru.

Those who participated in my Facebook Live during the infamous Covid summer of 2020. You helped me take this study to a new level.

First Baptist Church, Ellijay, Georgia. Especially all of you guys in Nancy Gheesling's sporty Sunday School class.

Front Range Alliance Church, Colorado Springs, Colorado. Especially Alicia Reeves and Beth Wahl for their sparkling insight.

Kristin Nave (*@shelovesbible*), Bible teacher, author, and founder of *All Things Bible*. Kristin, thanks for the encouragement and insights.

Chaplain Alicia Reeves and the offenders at La Vista Correctional Facility, Pueblo, Colorado.

Those who published books while I was on the long slog to completion. Your example helped me stay motivated. A shout-out this year to Col. Lee Ellis, Maj. Michelle (*Mace*) Curran, and Dr. Dane Egli.

About the Author

Dr. Sidney A. Webb received his master's and doctorate from Dallas Theological Seminary. He served as a veteran instructor with Walk Thru the Bible Ministries and has trained groups worldwide on everything from Bible overview to organizational governance.

Dr. Webb has spoken for organizations such as Walk Thru the Bible, Christian Leadership Alliance, Every Home for Christ, and The Voice of the Martyrs. He was also a leader in the "released time" education movement in the US and has served churches as Interim Pastor.

Sid and his wife Susan live in Colorado Springs and have been married for 45 years. In June 2013, the Black Forest wildfire destroyed their home and office. He published *Nomad's Fire: Life at the Intersection of Loss and Significance* to share their journey and challenge us to think about what matters most in life.

To have Dr. Webb speak to your church or group, or for more information, contact him at info@sharpenedfocus.com or the contact page on www.sharpenedfocus.com.

Other Books By Dr. Sidney A. Webb

Nomad's Fire: Life at the Intersection of Loss and Significance

The Goldilocks Board

Predictors of Understanding of the Duties of Care among Georgia Released Time Program Governing Board Members

Made in United States
Troutdale, OR
08/23/2023

12313360R00146